WRITER-FILES

General Editor: Simon Trussler

Associate Editor: Malcolm Page

File on
WILDE

Compiled by Margery Morgan

Methuen Drama

A Methuen Drama Book
First published in 1990 as a paperback original
by Methuen Drama, Michelin House,
81 Fulham Road, London SW3 6RB,
and HEB Inc., 70 Court Street, Portsmouth,
New Hampshire 03801, USA

Typeset in 9/10 Times by
L. Anderson Typesetting,
Woodchurch, Kent TN26 3TB

Printed in Great Britain
by Cox & Wyman Ltd, Reading

ISBN 0-413-53630-0

British Library Cataloguing in Publication Data
is available from the British Library

Contents

The theatre is, by its nature, an ephemeral art: yet it is a daunting task to track down the newspaper reviews, or contemporary statements from the writer or his director, which are often all that remain to help us recreate some sense of what a particular production was like. This series is therefore intended to make readily available a selection of the comments that the critics made about the plays of leading modern dramatists at the time of their production — and to trace, too, the course of each writer's own views about his work and his world.

In addition to combining a uniquely convenient source of such elusive *documentation*, the 'Writer-Files' series also assembles the *information* necessary for readers to pursue further their interest in a particular writer or work. Variations in quantity between one writer's output and another's, differences in temperament which make some readier than others to talk about their work, and the variety of critical response, all mean that the presentation and balance of material shifts between one volume and another: but we have tried to arrive at a format for the series which will nevertheless enable users of one volume readily to find their way around any other.

Section 1, 'A Brief Chronology', provides a quick conspective overview of each playwright's life and career. *Section 2* deals with the plays themselves, arranged chronologically in the order of their composition: information on first performances, major revivals, and publication is followed by a brief synopsis (for quick reference set in slightly larger, italic type), then by a representative selection of the critical response, and of the dramatist's own comments on the play and its theme.

Section 3 offers concise guidance to each writer's work in non-dramatic forms, while *Section 4*, 'The Writer on His Work', brings together comments from the playwright himself on more general matters of construction, opinion, and artistic development. Finally, *Section 5* provides a bibliographical guide to other primary and secondary sources of further reading, among which full details will be found of works cited elsewhere under short titles, and of collected editions of the plays — but not of individual titles, particulars of which will be found with the other factual data in Section 2.

The 'Writer-Files' hope by striking this kind of balance between information and a wide range of opinion to offer 'companions' to the study of major playwrights in the modern repertoire — not in that dangerous pre-digested fashion which

General Editor's Introduction

can too readily quench the desire to read the plays themselves, nor so prescriptively as to allow any single line of approach to predominate, but rather to encourage readers to form their own judgements of the plays in a wide-ranging context.

Oscar Wilde, who believed that art should shape life, had to suffer his own art being overwhelmed by his life. From the nice aesthetic debates and exquisitely wrought epigrams of his salad days to the criminal court and the prison cell of his decline, he traced, nevertheless, a kind of formal progression — from a figure proud to be parodied in comic opera, to one half way between pathos and tragedy as death overtook him in poverty and exile. The melodrama, in art and in life, came in between — in plays which now lean heavily on the reputation of his last and greatest dramatic sport, *The Importance of Being Earnest*.

Yet this in its way is also a period piece — an elegant, *fin de siècle* pantomime in which dramatic convention is elevated to the status of art while language is elevated to the condition of life. It is ironic that *Earnest* has come to be regarded as an easy option for unambitious amateur and student groups: for, as Wilde himself declared in the interview excerpted on page 43, 'we should treat all the trivial things of life very seriously'. The obverse, of course, was that 'all the serious things of life' should be treated 'with sincere and studied triviality'. The English are quite good at this, but only within limits strictly defined, both socially and sexually. Thus, Wilde might have achieved an even greater success than his compatriot and close contemporary Bernard Shaw had he, too, only learned how to avoid what the English declare off-limits. For the more liberal sections of Wilde's public, even homo-sexuality might have been acceptable as the topic of, well, an *earnest* if unperformable problem play: but it was not to be countenanced in the flamboyant life-style of a decadent dandy who insisted on flouting the English love of moderation, and fell victim to being 'too clever by half'.

Wilde, who revelled in paradox, claimed that the critic was a better artist than the artist himself, since he reduced the chaos of art to its essential elements, while the artist merely organized the chaos of life. But academic critics of his work have only recently begun to treat his trivialities with the degree of seriousness (as distinct, hopefully, from solemnity) they deserve. Theatre reviewers have done him more con-tinuous albeit pragmatic justice, and so are well represented in this volume. Yet much of Wilde's work — not just the plays, but the rich variety of non-dramatic writing here also surveyed — remains enig-matic, as if waiting for its time to come. Perhaps our own *fin de siècle* will better recognize its virtues — and be better able to relate them to the 'vices' by which the old 'nineties set limits to its naughtiness.

Simon Trussler

1854 16 Oct., born at 21 Westland Row, Dublin, second legitimate son of William Robert Wilde, physician and surgeon, and Jane Elgee, Irish nationalist poet known by *nom de plume*, 'Speranza'. His father was strongly Protestant, his mother had Catholic sympathies. Christened, in Protestant ritual, Oscar Fingal O'Flahertie Wills Wilde.

1855 The Wilde family moved to fashionable Merrion Square, Dublin, where Speranza started a *salon*. Oscar and his elder brother, Willie, had a French nurse and, later, a German governess and thus grew up speaking both foreign languages.

1858 Birth of sister, Isola.

1864 Father knighted, after his appointment as Surgeon Oculist to the Queen. Oscar and Willie were sent to Portora School, Enniskillen, where his interest in classical Greek and Latin literature developed. Lady Wilde won libel case brought by a patient who had accused Sir William of raping her.

1867 Isola died.

1870 Oscar won Carpenter Prize for Greek Testament studies.

1871 Entered Trinity College, Dublin. 10 Nov., Sir William's two illegitimate daughters, Emily (born 1847) and Mary (born 1849), were burnt to death. They and his illegitimate son, Henry (born 1838), are believed to have spent their summers with the legitimate family.

1873 Awarded a T.C.D. Foundation Scholarship.

1874 Won Berkeley Gold Medal for Greek. Did not sit final examination, but took (and excelled in) scholarship examination for Magdalen College, Oxford. Oct., went up to Oxford. Attended Ruskin's lectures and joined in his idealistic road-building activities at Hinksey. Already well-known for his aesthetic pose.

1875 Joined a Masonic Lodge. Came close to conversion to Roman Catholicism. Vacation travels in Italy. Began courtship of Florence Balcombe.

1876 April, death of Sir William Wilde. Despite his neglect of some courses, Wilde gained First Class in Honours Moderations (second year examinations).

1877 Prolonged vacation in Greece with Professor Mahaffy of T.C.D., returning *via* Rome. Rusticated for six months because of late arrival back in Oxford. This period was spent in London. July, first article published, 'The Grosvenor Gallery', in *Dublin University Magazine*. Meeting with Walter Pater, on return to Oxford. Writing long poem, *The Sphinx*, begun in 1874.

1878 His poem, *Ravenna*, won the Newdigate Prize. Gained a double first in Final Schools examination. Dec., Florence Balcombe married Bram Stoker (Henry Irving's manager and author of *Dracula*).

1879 Having failed to get a Classical Fellowship at Oxford, Wilde concentrated on London intellectual and political society, developing a friendship with Lillie Langtry and getting to know Ellen Terry, Sarah Bernhardt, and other leading actresses. Lady Wilde moved to London.

1880 Sept., sent Ellen Terry a copy of his first play, *Vera*.

1881 Moved to Tite Street, Chelsea, where Whistler was a neighbour. Satirized as Reginald Bunthorne in Gilbert and Sullivan's 'aesthetic' comic opera, *Patience*, produced in both London and New York. Volume of *Poems* published in England and America. Rehearsals of *Vera* cancelled because of politically sensitive situation.

1882 Jan.-May, lecture tour of USA. Returning to England, he met Constance Lloyd. May, started second tour of USA and Canada. (Wilde lectured on 'The English Renaissance', 'The House Beautiful', and 'The Decorative Arts'.) Writing *The Duchess of Padua*.

1883 Aug., production of *Vera* in USA. Went to Paris, where he met painters, writers, actors, etc., in a crowded social life. Much in the company of Robert Sherard.

1884 29 May, marriage to Constance Lloyd. Honeymoon in Paris. Wilde read Huysmans' *A Rebours* on its first appearance.

1885 The couple settled in a house in Tite Street, expensively decorated by E. W. Godwin. This left them in debt. Criminal Law Amendment Act passed, prohibiting homosexual acts between consenting male adults. 20 Feb., Whistler's Ten O'Clock Lecture, attacking

Wilde, who replied in two articles in *Pall Mall Gazette*. 5 June, birth of Cyril Wilde. On visits to Cambridge and Oxford, Oscar's attachments to young men became more marked.

1886   Met Robert Ross, then 17, in Oxford. According to Ross, this was Wilde's first homosexual affair. 5 Nov., birth of Vyvyan Wilde.

1887   May, assumed editorship of *The Lady's World*, changing the journal's title to *The Woman's World* and raising its quality. Wrote many reviews.

1888   Attended meetings of socialist Fabian Society. May, published *The Happy Prince and Other Tales*.

1889   Jan., 'Pen, Pencil and Poison' appeared in *Fortnightly Review* and 'The Decay of Lying' in *The Nineteenth Century*. Gave up editorship of *The Woman's World*.

1890   July and Sept., 'The Critic as Artist' published in *The Nineteenth Century*. Involved in a homosexual affair with poet (later priest), John Gray.

1891   *The Duchess of Padua* presented in USA, under the title *Guido Ferranti*, without an author's name. Published two volumes of stories, a book of critical essays (*Intentions*), his novel *The Picture of Dorian Gray*, and 'The Soul of Man under Socialism' in the *Fortnightly Review*. Wrote *Lady Windermere's Fan* and much of *Salomé* (in French). About late June, introduced to Lord Alfred Douglas by Lionel Johnson. July, first meeting with Aubrey Beardsley, who was to illustrate *Salomé*.

1892   Production of *Lady Windermere's Fan*. *Salomé* banned from public performance in England.

1893   Production of *A Woman of No Importance*.

1894   *An Ideal Husband* finished. *A Florentine Tragedy* and most of *La Sainte Courtisane* written. *The Sphinx* published. Aug.-Oct., writing *The Importance of Being Earnest* while at Worthing with Constance and their sons. Some of Wilde's letters to Lord Alfred Douglas came into the hands of Douglas's father, the Marquess of Queensberry. Sept., publication of Robert Hichens's scandalous novel, *The Green Carnation*, based on the Wilde circle.

1895   3 Jan., production of *An Ideal Husband* opened. 14 Feb.,

Queensberry's planned demonstration against Wilde, at the first performance of *The Importance of Being Earnest*, was foiled by the actor-manager, George Alexander. 28 Feb., insulting note from Queensberry delivered to Wilde at the Albemarle Club. 1 Mar., urged on by 'Bosie' (Alfred Douglas), Wilde brought a libel charge against Queensberry. 7 Mar., Oscar, Constance, and 'Bosie' went to see *The Importance of Being Earnest*. 3 Apr., hearings in libel case opened at the Old Bailey. Queensberry had been pursuing evidence against Wilde, and police information had built up, with the result that it was Wilde's guilt, rather than Queensberry's, that emerged in court. Apr., warrant issued for the arrest of Wilde, who still resisted the urgings of friends — but not 'Bosie' — that he should slip away to France. His name was subsequently removed from advertisement hoardings outside the theatres where his plays were being performed. 24 Apr., Wilde was declared bankrupt, and his possessions were sold. 26 Apr., the trial opened. When the Jury did not agree on a verdict, a new trial was ordered. 25 May, sentenced to two years' imprisonment with hard labour. Taken to Newgate, thence to Holloway, and from there to Pentonville Gaol; then moved to Wandsworth, where he injured his ear in a fall. Books were supplied to him, following the intervention of R. B. Haldane. 8 Sept., Constance decided against a divorce. 21 Nov., transfer to Reading Gaol. More books supplied, but he was still not allowed to write.

1896 11 Feb., Lugné-Poë presented *Salomé* at Théâtre de l'Oeuvre in Paris. 19 Feb., Constance visited her husband, bringing news of Lady Wilde's death on 3 Feb. July, appointment of a new, more humane warden at Reading. Oscar was allowed writing materials. He began to study Italian and German systematically and to write *De Profundis* in the form of a long letter to Alfred Douglas. 19 May, released from prison. 20 May, travelled to Dieppe, where he handed Robert Ross the manuscript of *De Profundis* for copying, and began life as Sebastian Melmoth with £800 raised by Ross from subscriptions.

1897 July-Aug., wrote and revised *The Ballad of Reading Gaol* (later expanded). Aug.-Dec., with Alfred Douglas in France and Italy.

1898 9 Feb., Leonard Smithers published *The Ballad of Reading Gaol*, which went into many reprints. (That of June 1899 was the first to carry Wilde's name on the title page, not just his cell number.) Publication of *The Importance of Being Earnest* and *An Ideal Husband* followed. Apr., Constance died, following an operation on her spine. (She and the boys had adopted the surname Holland.)

1899   Death of Willie Wilde. (The brothers had been estranged for some years.)

1900   1 Jan., Queensberry died, leaving £20,000 to Alfred Douglas, who refused any financial help to Wilde. Some months later, George Alexander offered to make voluntary payments on performances of Wilde's plays and to bequeathe the copyright to Wilde's sons. 30 Nov., Oscar Wilde died in Paris, having been baptised into the Catholic Church. He had been virtually destitute and much alone in the final years, and had not succeeded in writing anything of substance. He never broke completely with Alfred Douglas, who paid for his funeral.

1905   Ross published *De Profundis* in abridged form, and presented the complete manuscript to the British Museum. (It became available to the public in 1960.)

1906   Through Ross's efforts, the Wilde estate was discharged from bankruptcy.

1910   Wilde was re-buried at the cemetery of Père Lachaise. (A monument by Epstein was erected at his grave in 1912.)

a: Stage Plays

Vera, or The Nihilists.

A drama in a prologue and four acts.
Written: *c*. 1879-80; revised for production, 1883.
First production: Union Square Th., New York, 20 Aug. 1883 and subsequently on tour (prod. Marie Prescott, who played heroine).
First English production: Globe Th., 1 July 1890.
Revived: by amateurs, Durham, *c*. 26 Jan. 1956.
Published: privately, 1880; revised acting edition, 1882. *First published separately*: ed. Frances Miriam Reed, Lewiston, N.Y.: Edwin Mellen Press, 1989. In *Collected Works*; *Complete Plays*, Methuen, p. 515-78.

A Prologue establishes Vera's original motivation: as daughter of a village innkeeper, she sees her brother Dimitri among prisoners in chains on their way from Moscow to Siberia under armed guard, and her father — who normally professes indifference to the fate of others — collapses when his attempt at self-sacrifice fails. Act I, some time later, presents Vera as leader of a band of Nihilists meeting at the Moscow address her brother had smuggled to her. She returns from a ball at the Czar's palace, which she entered in disguise, with news of an imminent declaration of martial law. The conspirators are shown as masqueraders in their own way, and Michael Strogoff (who seems to be Vera's old suitor from the village, unrecognized here) believes they have a royalist spy in their own midst: Alexis, whose loyalty Vera defends. When General Kotemkin arrives with soldiers, Alexis saves his comrades by tearing off his mask to reveal that he is the Czarevitch and supporting the others' claim to be a band of strolling players. Act II, in a Council Chamber at the Palace, introduces the Prime Minister, Prince Paul, who is a Wildean sophisticated aesthete, and the Czar, neurotic with fear. Prince Paul is amused by the paradox of a socialist Czarevitch, but anticipates that the imperial crown will convert him. The test is at hand, as a shot from the crowd kills the Czar on the balcony. Act III, back in the Nihilists' house, proceeds in a kind of travesty of Act I, with the Fifth Conspirator unmasking to reveal himself as Prince Paul, but claiming to be a genuine convert. When Alexis fails to appear he is judged to be a traitor and condemned to die. The task of killing the young Czar falls to Vera (who loves him), and the act ends with her self-dedication to regicide. Act IV takes place in a palace antechamber, where the crown lies symbolically on the table. We hear of reformist measures decreed by the new Czar, and he banishes his ministers (another conspiratorial group). He sleeps, having sent his guards and page away. When Vera enters to stab him, he fails to notice her dagger, but declares his love for her. Vera's resolve breaks in a liebestod. She stabs herself with the poisoned dagger, then throws it out of the window (a prearranged signal of her success) before Alexis can do the same. Her last words, 'I have saved Russia', are appropriately ambiguous.

I send you a copy of my first play. . . . Its literary merit is very slight, but in an acting age perhaps the best test of a good play is that it should not read well. . . . I think the second act is good writing and the fourth good position — but how hard to know the value of one's own work!

Wilde, to E.F.S. Pigott
(Examiner of Plays for the Lord Chamberlain),
Sept. 1880, in *More Letters*, p. 32

I send you the prologue: if it is too long cut it. I have introduced Prince Paul Maraloffski in it as a simple Colonel: this will give a dramatic point to his meeting Vera among the Nihilists in the third act, where I will introduce a little speech about it. . . . The first act, which at present stands 'Tomb of the Kings at Moscow', has too operatic a title: it is to be called '99 Rue Tchernavaza, Moscow', and the conspirators are to be *modern*, and the room a bare garret, painted crimson. It is to be realistic not operatic conspiracy.

Wilde, to Richard D'Oyly Carte, March 1882,
in *Letters*, p. 104

I have tried in it to express within the limits of art that Titan cry of the peoples for liberty, which in the Europe of our day is threatening thrones, and making governments unstable from Spain to Russia. . . . But it is a play not of politics but of passion. It deals with no theories of government, but with men and women simply; and modern Nihilistic Russia, with all the terror of its tyranny and the marvel of its martyrdoms, is merely the fiery and fervent background in front of which the persons of my dream live and love. . . .

Wilde, to Marie Prescott, c. July 1883,
in *Letters*, p. 148-9

Vera is a prose play in five acts, which I wrote seven years ago. It was not produced in England because its political sentiments would not have found favour there. . . . I have chosen the most extreme expression of liberty, the Nihilism of Russia, which is akin to the anarchism of old France. All art takes an aristocratic view of life, for civilization belongs to the higher classes. I want to show how far the aspirations of an uncultivated people can be made a subject for art. . . . The incidents are purely imaginary, with modern Russia as the realistic background. . . . The drama is . . . the great democratic art. I wanted to see if I could write a play which would satisfy not merely artists but the people.

Wilde, interviewed for *The World* (New York), 12 Aug. 1883,
reprinted in Mikhail, *Interviews and Recollections*, I, p. 115

Mr. Wilde believes, apparently, that Nihilism is an imposing force of the age. At any rate, he does not see the serious side of it. . . . The fine poetic charm and the strength of the final situation redeem, one is almost willing to say, the other four acts of *Vera*. Yet this would be saying too much. The Nihilism which is presented in *Vera* is a stupid and tiresome element of the work. These rabid fellows who talk like lunatics, swear the most preposterous oaths, and act like children give no dramatic force to the play. It should be observed clearly that they do not act — they talk. They yell their theories of liberty. They argue and quarrel. The monotony of the second and fourth acts of *Vera* is simply depressing. . . . In the third act the Czar and his son have a vivacious dispute, which carries on the particular argumentative purpose of the play. . . . Mr. Wilde's play is, in fact, an energetic tirade against tyrants and despots. . . . But . . . *Vera* is not dramatic. Yet there is constantly suggested in it a dramatic motive which is not shown concretely. The first act or prologue, for example, opens well as an exposition. It is then felt that the drama lies between Vera and Alexis, in their love and tragic passions. But the body of the play does not exhibit this drama, which appears only in the last act. . . . There is a great deal of good writing in *Vera*, and Mr. Wilde exhibits cleverness and wit in a character like Prince Paul. . . .

Unsigned review, <i>New York Times</i>, 21 Aug. 1883,
reprinted in Beckson, <i>Critical Heritage: Wilde</i>, p. 55-61

Undergraduate actors are turning more and more to the production of plays that lie outside the usual range of professional theatre and are yet of interest to students of dramatic or stage history. Durham University literary and debating society is this week bringing out into the light again a play more than usually obscure, Oscar Wilde's *Vera, or The Nihilists*.

It has claims to attention as being unlike anything else by its author. It is pure melodrama . . . with its heroine turning nihilist for sentimental reasons rather than out of political convictions, and torn between her duty to the cause and her love for the Czarevitch Alexander, a nihilist by conviction. . . . Wilde risks the repetition of an important effect, since the unmasking of the Czarevitch in one act is paralleled in another by that of the villain of the piece, Prince Paul, the cynical former Prime Minister and the late Czar's evil genius, who has also joined the nihilists in order to revenge himself on Alexander. . . .

The Times, 27 Jan. 1956

The Duchess of Padua

Blank verse tragedy in five acts.
Written: 1883.
First production: under title, *Guido Ferranti*, Broadway Th., New York, 26 Jan. 1891 (produced by Lawrence Barrett, who played Guido, with Frederic Vroom as the Duke, Minna K. Gale as Beatrice, John Lane as Moranzone).
First German production: 1904; revived 1906 and subsequently.
First English production, to establish copyright: St. James's Th., 18 March 1907.
First published: in authorized German translation by Dr. Max Meyerfeld, as *Der Herzogin von Padua*, Berlin: Egon Fleischel, 1904.
First published in English: Paris: Charles Carrington, 1905. (A pirated version in prose based on the German edition, claiming to have been published in New York.)
First publication in English verse: Collected Works, ed. Ross, London: Methuen, 1908 (from an acting text with Wilde's manuscript corrections). In *Complete Plays*, Methuen, p. 415-515.

The setting is Padua in the later sixteenth century. Guido Ferranti is urged by the mysterious Lord Moranzone to avenge his (unknown) father's death on Duke Lorenzo. Guido accepts this as his duty, only to have his dagger slip from his hand at first glimpse of the Duchess. Act II contrasts the goodness of the Duchess with the tyrannical cruelty of her husband, who is also this play's sophisticated ironist. What is virtually a love-duet between Guido and the Duchess ends with a reminder from the sinister Moranzone. Seeing the incompatibility of vengeance and love, Guido renounces the Duchess, who thereupon plans suicide. The twists and turns of the plot reflect both Hamlet *and* Romeo and Juliet. *Guido vacillates, but the Duke is murdered by his Duchess. Guido is arrested, brought to trial, and takes the guilt upon himself. The last act is set in a cell, where the Duchess visits Guido. She drinks the poison meant for him, and Guido stabs himself with her dagger.*

The author of *Guido Ferranti*, the sombre romantic play produced at the Broadway Theatre last night by Mr. Lawrence Barrett, has a gift . . . of melody. If he is, indeed, a poet, he is probably at his best in writing lyrics. His five-act play is not altogether poetical. A dramatic poet who is equal to his task is not compelled to seek in the graveyard of dead forms of speech for phrases and metaphors. There are lots of reminiscent lines in *Guido Ferranti* . . . there is an oath of vengeance that is a reminder of a dozen almost forgotten tragedies, but there are some passages full of the fire of eloquence. . . . The authorship of *Guido Ferranti* has been attributed by a competent authority to Oscar Wilde. It is said that Mr. Wilde wrote the play ten years ago or more, and that it was then called *The Duchess of Padua*. . . .

The manner of this work is, as we have said, better than the ordinary. If we are sometimes reminded of Sheridan Knowles, we are, nevertheless, more frequently reminded of Browning. The author. . . does not live wholly in the past. There are a number of well-imagined and skilfully wrought scenes in his play, and many passages that must have been written in a glow of excitement.

Unsigned review, *New York Times*, 27 Jan. 1891

Salomé

A tragedy in one act.

Written: in French, 1881.

First production in original French: Théâtre de l'Oeuvre, 11 Feb. 1896 (prod. Lugné-Poë, who also played Herod).

First production in German: private matinee, Kleines Theater, Berlin, 22 Feb. 1902 (dir. Max Reinhardt); revived Kleines Theater, 15 Nov. 1902; trans. Neues Theater, 29 Sept. 1903.

First private production in English: Bijou Th., London, 10 May 1905 (New Stage Club, dir. Florence Farr, with Robert Farquharson). The play was banned from public performance in England until 1930.

First American production: Berkeley Lyceum Th., New York, 13 Nov. 1905 (Progressive Stage Society).

Revived: King's Hall, London, 10 June 1906 (Literary Theatre Society, dir. and des. Charles Ricketts, with Robert Farquharson, Florence Darragh, and Lewis Casson as Jokanaan), then at National Sporting Club, 20 June 1906; New German Th., New York, 23 March 1909 (in German); Court Th., London, 27 and 28 Feb. 1911 (private perf. by New Players, dir. Harcourt Williams, with Adeline Bourne, Edyth Olive, Arthur Wontner and Eric Maturin); Comedy Th., New York, 21 Dec. 1913 (in Italian); Punch and Judy Th., New York, 7 March 1916 (in German); Comedy Th., New York, 22 April 1918 (Washington Square Players); Court Th., 12 Apr. 1911 (Independent Th. Co., with Maud Allen as Salomé); Tokyo, 1919 (des. Charles Ricketts); Klaw Th., New York, 22 May 1922 (Players' Forum); Frazee Th., New York, 7 May 1923 (Ethiopian Art Theatre); Gate Th., Dublin, 12 Dec. 1928 (with Micheál MacLiammoir as Jokanaan, Hilton Edwards as Herod); Festival Th., Cambridge, 9 June 1929 (private perf., dir. Terence Gray, des. Gray and Doria Paston, with Vivienne Bennett and George Colouris); Gate Th., London, 27 May 1931 (adapted Constant Lambert, dir. Peter Godfrey, choreographed Ninette de Valois, with Robert Speaight as Herod, John Clements as Jokaanan, Margaret Rawlings as Salomé, Flora Robson as Herodias); Festival Th., Cambridge, 23 Nov. 1931 (dir. Terence Gray, des. Gray and Paston, with Constant Lambert's score, dance choreographed Ninette de Valois, other movement devised by Hedley Briggs, with Beatrix Lehmann as Salomé, and Robert Morley as Herod); Savoy Th., 5 Oct. 1931 (dir. Nancy Price, who also played Herodias, with Robert Speaight as Herod, Joan Maude as Salomé, Robert Donat as the Young Syrian); Th. in the Dale, New Milford, Conn., 5 Aug. 1946 (with Tilly Losch as Salomé); Rudolf Steiner Th., London, 1 May 1947 (Centaur Th. Co.); New Torch Th., London, 20 May 1952 (dir. Ronald Lane, with Richmond Naime as Herod, Prudence Hyman as Salomé); Q Th., 15 June 1954 (dir. Frederick Farley, with Frank Thring as Herod, Agnes Bernelle as Salomé, Vivienne Bennett as Herodias), trans. St. Martin's Th.,

20 July 1954 (with John Schlesinger and Ronald Harwood as anonymous Jews); Th. le Globe MCDV, Paris, 1972 (in French, with all-male cast); Truck and Warehouse Theatres, 6 Jan. 1975 (New York Theatre Ensemble, adapted, dir. and des. Lindsay Kemp, who also played Salomé, music composed by William Hellermann, with David Meyer as Herod, Incredible Orlando as Herodias); Lyceum Th., Edinburgh, from Gate Th., Dublin, 13 Aug. 1989 (dir. Steven Berkoff), trans. Lyttelton Th., 5 Oct. 1989.

Opera: Wilde's play was used as libretto for Richard Strauss's *Salomé*, first produced Metropolitan Opera House, New York, 13 Nov. 1905; first produced in England at Covent Garden, 8 Dec. 1910, by Beecham Opera Co. More frequently revived than the original play.

First published: in French, Paris: Librairie de l'Art Indépendant; London: Elkin Mathews and John Lane, 1893; in English, translated from the French (probably Wilde's own revision of Alfred Douglas's translation), and illus. by Aubrey Beardsley, London: Elkin Mathews and John Lane; Boston: Copeland and Day, 1894. French text in *Collected Works*, 1908, repr. 1927; English text in *Complete Plays*, Methuen, p. 379-414.

Films: William Fox silent screen version, with Theda Bara, 1918; a second silent version, an attempt to animate the book, with Beardsley's designs, directed by Charles Bryant for Nazimova, who played Salomé. (Halliwell quotes the *New Yorker*, 1980: 'looks better in stills than when one actually sees it, but a folly like this should probably be experienced'.)

The innocent young Salomé, daughter of Queen Herodias, falls passionately in love with the prisoner Jokanaan, a dedicated ascetic who spurns her. King Herod, obsessed with her beauty, offers her whatever she may desire if only she will dance for him. In the confusion of her feelings, she asks for — and is ultimately granted — Jokanaan's head on a silver charger. When, at the end of her dance, she kisses the dead mouth, Herod's soldiers crush her beneath their shields.

The pleasure and pride that I have experienced in the whole affair has been that Madame Sarah Bernhardt . . . should have been charmed and fascinated by my play and she should have wished to act it. . . . Every rehearsal . . . has been a source of intense pleasure to me. To hear my own words spoken by the most beautiful voice in the world has been the greatest artistic joy. . . . But there is a Censorship over the stage and acting, and the basis of that Censorship is that, while vulgar subjects may be put on the stage and acted, . . . no actor is to be permitted to present under artistic conditions, the great and ennobling subjects taken from the Bible. The insult in the suppression of *Salomé*, is an insult to the stage as a form of art. . . .

> Wilde, interview reported in *Pall Mall Budget*, 30 June 1892
> (on the occasion of the Lord Chamberlain's banning of a planned
> London production by and with Sarah Bernhardt),
> reprinted in Mikhail, *Interviews and Recollections*, I, p. 186-7

'How came you to write *Salomé* in French?'
. . . I have one instrument that I know that I can command, and that is the English language. There was another instrument to which I had listened all my life, and I wanted once to touch this new instrument to see whether I could make any beautiful thing out of it. . . . A great deal of the curious effect that Maeterlinck produces comes from the fact that he, a Flamand by grace, writes in an alien language.

> Wilde, as above, p. 188

There were ten, no a hundred Salomés that he imagined, that he began, that he abandoned. Each painting he saw in a museum suggested a new idea; each book he found in which the object of his interest was mentioned filled him with self-doubt. One day his princess was blonde and extolled herself like Mallarmé's Salomé. . . . The next day Wilde would hurry to consult the Gospels. . . . But Wilde found this story dry and colourless; without lavishness, extravagance or sin. Above all, sin. To become the supreme incarnation of sexual love, this poor girl who obeys her mother, receives the blood-stained gift, and presents it, must have the dreams and visions of men heaped about her feet for centuries. . . .

> Gomez Carrillo, 'Comment Oscar Wilde rêva Salomé',
> *La Plume*, Paris, 1902; in English translation,
> Mikhail, *Interviews and Recollections*, I, p. 194-5

In September, new scenes occurred, the occasion of them being my pointing out the schoolboy faults of your attempted translation of *Salomé*. You must by this time be a fair enough French scholar to know that the translation was as unworthy of you, as an ordinary Oxonian, as it was of the work it sought to render.

> Wilde, to Lord Alfred Douglas (*De Profundis*),
> in *Letters*, p. 431-2

I do not claim it [*the published English version*] as my translation. I think my own translation, as a matter of fact, was better.

Alfred Douglas, *A Summing Up*

It is one of the refrains whose recurring *motifs* make *Salomé* so like a piece of music and bind it together as a ballad.

Wilde, *De Profundis*, in *Letters*, p. 475

[*On Max Reinhardt's production*] A performance famed for its sensuous interpretation, its high tension and optical innovations. (For the first time, three-dimensional sets — designed by Max Kruse — were employed, giving the tiny stage an unwonted depth and leaving much more to the audience's imagination than met its eye. But, more crucial, it was the first time that the art of the actress Gertrud Eysoldt came into bloom in the title role, shocking and exhilarating Berlin with her electric emotional charge, exploding uninhibitedly.)

Gottfried Reinhardt, *The Genius: a Memoir of Max Reinhardt* (New York: Knopf, 1979), p. 345

The production was chiefly memorable for the opportunity it lent the painter Louis Corinth and the sculptor Max Kruse, who designed the exotic costumes and settings in period. The sultry atmosphere and mid-Eastern sensuality were captured in transparent draperies, and Reinhardt experimented with sky-blue silk against a high cyclorama, lit by the new Fortuny system of indirect lighting, together with a spotlight to create the effect of moonlight.

J. L. Styan, *Max Reinhardt* (Cambridge University Press, 1982), p. 25-6

The English translation of [*Salomé*] was performed last Wednesday at the Bijou Theatre, Bayswater. . . . Mr. Wilde was a born dramatist — a born theatrist, too, Not less than in his handling of the quick and complex form of modern comedy, there was mastery in his handling of this slow and simple form of tragedy — a form compounded, seemingly, of Sophocles and Maeterlinck in even proportions. The note of terror in *Salomé* is struck well in the opening lines, and then slowly the play's action advances, step by step, to the foreknown crisis; and it is mainly through this very slowness, this constant air of suspense, that the play yields us the tragic thrill. . . . Certainly it is a good 'stage play' so far as the technique of its author is concerned. But, for all that, it is not a good play for the stage. It is too horrible for definite and corporeal presentment. . . . Here, indeed, was Herod himself, incarnate from out the pages of the play — a terrible being, half-dotard, half-child, corrupt with all the corruptions of the world, and yet not without certain dark remnants of the intellect, of dignity. I do not remember that I had ever before seen Mr. Robert Farquharson (for he it was). . . . Passages that might have been merely beautiful he made dramatically hideous, without loss of their beauty. Passages that might have been merely hideous he made beautiful, without loss of their appropriateness. Of course he played all the other people off the stage, figuratively. Literally, they remained there, I regret to say.

Max Beerbohm, *Saturday Review*, 13 May 1905;
reprinted in *Around Theatres*, p. 140-4

June 10 [1906]. Turned up at four, nailed up scenery . . . placed furniture, supervised dresses: train of Salomé lost, dress for Bianca [in *Florentine Tragedy*] lost in building . . . ; rehearsed taking of head with Miss Darragh, who grew nervous; stood by the limelight man, the most absolute idiot I have met in my life. Audience enthusiastic. Three calls at the end of the *Florentine Tragedy*, four at the end of *Salomé*. . . . Dance begun too soon, over too soon. Salomé missed covering the head of St. John with a veil.

June 16. Rehearsal in morning. News of boycott by Press, *The Times* returned the ticket. No illustrated paper will publish the photographs.

June 18. Theatre at eleven with lute, etc. See scenery. Performance was taken at too slow a pace. Two ladies left the house in large hats. Shaw watched it intently. Duse was so deeply veiled that I did not see her.

Charles Ricketts, *Self Portrait . . . from
the Letters and Journals*, collected and compiled by
T. Sturge Moore, ed. Cecil Lewis
(London: Peter Davies, 1939), p. 135

At the King's Hall, Miss Darragh . . . is not the ideal Salomé; for she looks rather modern, rather occidental. But, besides having a beautiful voice, and speaking the words with a keen sense for their cadence, she is a genuine tragedian, and thus was able . . . to purge somewhat our physical disgust through spiritual terror. She was, as nearly as need be, the veritable daughter of Herodias. Miss Florence Farr was not, alas, the veritable mother of Salomé. . . . She seemed to be trying to make Herodias 'sympathetic', and was quite out of the key of the tragedy. Mr. Robert Farquharson reappeared as Herod; and I was more than ever struck by the fineness of his performance. His delivery of the three long decorative speeches is a marvel in the art of elocution. . . . Mr. Farquharson can, without slurring a syllable, speak English as rapidly as Madame Sarah Bernhardt can speak French; and the effect in his case is even greater than in hers, because none of his compatriots has attempted to compete with him. Apart from its technique, his performance is memorable for the rare imaginative power with which he realizes the grotesque and terrible figure of Herod.

As the scenery and the dresses were designed by Mr. Charles Ricketts, it need not be said they were beautiful. They were also, however, dramatically appropriate — just enough conventionalized to be in harmony with the peculiar character of the play.

> Max Beerbohm, in *Saturday Review*, 16 June 1906;
> reprinted in *Last Theatres*, p. 250-1

The Gate Theatre . . . was a club, and therefore able to present plays that were considered too immoral to be exposed to the delicate sensibilities of a public theatre audience. One of these was Oscar Wilde's *Salomé*. . . . The incidental music — for clarinet, trumpet, cello and percussion — was by Lambert, and the small group who played it were placed on a shelf above the dressing-room. The cast had to get in early and shut the door so that a ladder could be propped between stage and orchestra; Lambert mounted the ladder and conducted while perched on one of the rungs. . . . The play ran for thirty-two performances. Lambert's score . . . is in nine movements, all very short except for the Dance. For this piece Lambert, like Strauss, wrote a fast, loud opening to attract attention; then the music became slow for a while and gradually gained speed until a hectic final *presto*.

> Richard Shead, *Constant Lambert*
> (London: Simon Publications, 1973), p. 89-90

The beauty of the gleaming silver columns and staircases (the entire set was coated with aluminium paint) against the dark blue sky, the massiveness accentuated by the purple light flooding the acting area, slowly degenerated . . . to a lurid decadence as first the vast red moon rose over the Tetrarch's throne and then garish lights filtered from his feast through the columns throwing contorted shadows . . . a superlatively conceived acting space in terms of the play . . . the Prophet's . . . monumental calm emphasized . . . by . . . giving the actor a mask.

> Richard Cave (commenting on slides),
> *Terence Gray and the Cambridge Festival Theatre*, p. 62-4

Few opportunities are given of seeing this beautifully decadent play, rich in a fantastic riot of language which our actors have forgotten how to use. . . . Its sources are obvious, particularly Flaubert and Maeterlinck in whose peculiar style it is an essay. . . . Frederick Farley's production is an odd example of the obviously theatrical without the distilled, haunting beauty which Wilde had in mind.

Salomé, as portrayed by Agnes Bernelle, lacks the vital sexual urge and the intelligence of [*sic*] expressing this urge through voice and movement. . . . This dance . . . was a particularly vulgar one, like a strip-tease at a bridge party. Vivienne Bennett's Herodias has authority, variety and a hard, jealous strength which adds much to the great climax.

Frank Thring as Herod gets nearest to the heart of the play with his forceful, cruel, voluptuous performance.

R[onald] B[arker], *Plays and Players*, Aug. 1954

The meditations on the strange half-bestial lovers of the Sphinx or on Salomé's passion for John the Baptist are auto-eroticism, not negative capability. There is no question of Wilde thinking himself into the soul of Salomé, understanding her motivation, suffering her passion; he is simply using Salomé imaginatively in order to experience a new *frisson*. And, when Herod turns at the end of the play and gives orders, 'Tuez cette femme', the act itself means nothing save that the reverie is over: Salomé has fulfilled her function.

Barbara Charlesworth, *Dark Passages*, p. 61

Lindsay Kemp has given a completely Wildean interpretation, effecting the transformation of a middle-aged, balding dancer into the young princess by the strength of his vision of the Salomé in himself. . . . When he abandoned all theatrical aids — glamorous costume, wig and so on — and performed the final sequence in his own person, he amazingly achieved that inner transformation and self-revelation with which Wilde was fundamentally concerned.

Katharine Worth, *Oscar Wilde*, p. 67

Berkoff . . . stages the play in 'twenties costume as a dinner-party taking place at Herod's house.

The Roman guests are rather like Bright Young Things peering down at the entombed Jokanaan as if he were some form of bizarre cabaret but finally reduced in the presence of death to gap-mouthed awe. (Berkoff . . . is good at crowds.) The tetchy Tetrarch presides over the feast like some incestuous corporate boss. Roger Doyle's piano music tinkles quietly in the background as if Satie had invaded the world of Erté.

Everything on stage is calculated, artificial, deliberate. The actors roll each syllable lasciviously round their tongues. They also glide in slow motion as if being filmed underwater by Jacques Cousteau. It works because it exactly matches the enclosed, symbolist dream-world that Wilde has created. And the actors have a strong enough individuality to avoid seeming like manipulated marionettes. . . .

What the show, which moves to the National Theatre later this year, proves is that Berkoff is a very good director. He gives us a controlled dream that, in its reigned-in eroticism and disciplined frenzy, suggests Wilde's tragedy is less a piece of Biblical exotica than a dramatized symbolist poem. He has, in fact, staged this drama of decapitation without losing his head.

Michael Billington, The Guardian, 16 Aug. 1989

Lady Windermere's Fan

A drama in four acts.

Written: 1891, provisionally titled *A Good Woman.*

First production: St. James's Th., 20 Feb. 1892 (prod. George Alexander, who played Lord Windermere, with Marion Terry as Mrs. Erlynne, Ben Webster as Cecil Graham); revived St. James's Th., 14 Oct. 1911.

Revived: Everyman Th., 3 July 1930 (dir. Stephen Thomas, with Eric Maturin as Lord Darlington, Cecil Parker as Lord Windermere, Ernest Thesiger as Dumby, George Merritt as Lord Augustus, Kate Cutler as Mrs. Erlynne, Margaret Yarde as Duchess of Berwick, Mary Hinton as Lady Plimdale); Haymarket Th., 21 Aug. 1945 (dir. John Gielgud, des. Cecil Beaton, with Athene Seyler as Duchess of Berwick, Griffith Jones as Lord Darlington, Isabel Jeans as Mrs. Erlynne, Denys Blakelock as Cecil Graham); Curran Th., San Francisco, 26 Aug. 1946 (des. Cecil Beaton, who also played Cecil Graham), trans. Cort Th., New York, Oct. 1946; Royal Th., Brighton, 23 Aug. 1966, trans. Phoenix Th., London, 13 Oct. 1966 (dir. Anthony Quayle, des. Cecil Beaton, with Juliet Mills as Lady Windermere, Ronald Lewis as Lord Darlington, Isabel Jeans as Duchess of Berwick, Wilfred Hyde White as Lord Augustus, Coral Browne as Mrs. Erlynne, Corin Redgrave as Cecil Graham).

First published: London: Elkin Mathews and John Lane, 1893.

Most authoritative text: New Mermaid edition, 1980.

Musical versions: Noel Coward's *After the Ball*, first performed Globe Th., 10 June 1954; *A Delightful Season*, first performed Gramercy Arts Th., USA, 1960.

Films: Warner Bros., 1925 (silent, dir. Ernst Lubitsch, with Ronald Colman, Irene Rich. 'Oscar Wilde's play transposed to the 'twenties, with the Lubitsch touch daringly displacing Wildean epigrams', *Halliwell's Film Guide*); *The Fan*, U S 1949 (Wilde's title restored in Britain; dir. Otto Preminger, script Walter Reisch, Dorothy Parker, and Ross Evans, with George Sanders, Madeleine Carroll, Jeanne Craine, Richard Greene, Martita Hunt).

A fan, birthday gift from Lord Windermere to his young wife, lies on the morning-room table throughout Act I, a visual token of the themes of concealment and hypocrisy, but also of the deft, well-meaning politenesses essential to social life. Wilde achieves a re-definition of feminine goodness — demolishing Charles Kingsley's thoroughly Victorian opposition between 'good' and 'clever' ('Be good, sweet maid, and let who will be clever') — through the education of Lady Windermere by the experience of error and her rescue by a 'woman with a past', Mrs. Erlynne. Lady Windermere suspects her husband of having an affair with Mrs. Erlynne. His concern to keep her ignorant that the latter is, in truth, her mother, provokes Lady Windermere's flight from her birthday dance to the apartment of an admirer, Lord Darlington. His absence gives Mrs. Erlynne the opportunity to conceal what has happened, persuade Lady Windermere to return to her child, and, when Windermere and Augustus Lorton arrive with Darlington at his rooms, she emerges to claim the fan left behind by the other woman. The play ends on the note of comedy, with the Windermeres reconciled, and a marriage in prospect between Mrs. Erlynne and Lorton, who has accepted her ingenious explanation of all that has happened. Some part of the full truth remains hidden from each of the other main characters, to the comfort of all.

I heard by chance in the theatre today . . . that you intended using the first scene [set] a second time — in the last act. . . . If you are unable to give the play its full scenic mounting, the scene that has to be repeated should be *the second, not the first*. Lady Windermere may be in her drawing-room in the fourth act. *She should not be in her husband's library*. This is a very important point.

Now the advantages of using Scene ii are these:

25

In Act II the scene is night. The ballroom is open, and so is the terrace. In Act IV, the scene being day, the ballroom is closed, the windows shut, and the furniture can be differently arranged. . . .

And the disadvantage is a great one, because the scene — a vital one in the play — between the Duchess and Lady Windermere takes place on the sofa on the right of the stage. Now Mrs. Erlynne should not have her scene in the same place. It impoverishes the effect. . . . Mrs Erlynne should hold the centre of the stage and be its central figure. . . .

Windermere, being in his own house, can pace up and down — does, in fact, do so; Mrs. Erlynne, of course, cannot do anything of the kind. She rises from the sofa . . . and sits down, but with the possibility of Lady Windermere entering at any moment, for her to walk about . . . would be melodramatic, but not dramatic or artistic.

> Wilde, to George Alexander, Feb. 1892,
> in *More Letters*, p. 109-11

I feel sure that the author of this clever play must have regretted his rash and groundless statement that actors are mere puppets, and that interpretations are utterly subservient to creation, when he saw Winifred Emery play the sweet and childlike heroine in *Lady Windermere's Fan*. . . . She gave positively a new complexion to the play. She restored its lost balance; she gave just that power of innocence, that charm of nature, that rare ideality and womanliness which are the proper contrasts and antidotes to the cynicism, worldliness, and paradox which are the leading features of this complex work.

Winifred Emery rightly grasped the character and understood the dreaminess of Lady Windermere's nature. She stood before us as a woman instinctively refined and infinitely gentle. In the first act we saw a proud, thoughtful, religious woman, awakening, almost with a shudder, to the sorrows of society. The knowledge of sin is forced upon her; she is dragged against her will to its very gates. But the subtlest and most delicate features of Winifred Emery's acting were only seen in the scenes with Mrs. Erlynne — her mother — played to perfection by Marion Terry. Here she evidently desired to show us — and she did it most beautifully — the dim overshadowing influence of the mother who is by her side. She does not know it is her mother, but she feels she is under a mysterious spell.

At the conclusion of the great scene of the play, grandly acted by Marion Terry and Winifred Emery, there was an infinitely pathetic touch — just the touch that all cried out for when the play was first produced. It was the infinitely tender scene in the play when Lady Windermere breaks down at the mention of her child, and then, herself a child again, plaintively moans to the protecting mother, 'Take me home.' But this was no mere artist's point. It was part and parcel of Winifred Emery's conception. At the close of the play this gentle lady is still under the maternal spell; and whatever Mrs. Erlynne bids her do, that she does, awed as it were by the very presence of the woman she believes to be dead, the woman who is the subject of her nightly prayers.

Clement Scott, *The Drama of To-Day and Yesterday*
(London: Macmillan, 1899), Vol. II, p. 326-7

Whereas Maeterlinck made the theatre the cradle for his marvellous infancy — infancy, as it were, almost in the literal sense of speechlessness — . . . it was by way of a brilliant afterthought that Oscar Wilde began to be a playwright. Already he had, from time to time, touched, and adorned, all the literary modes — achieving, I think, his finest mastery in the forms of the fairy story and of the philosophic essay in dialogue. He found in the theatre a new diversion. He did not, at first, take the theatre seriously. He was content to express himself through the handiest current form of play. And that form happened to be Sardouesque comedy. It is inevitable, therefore, that *Lady Windermere's Fan* should seem to us, now that we see it again at the St James's Theatre, after the lapse of twelve years, old-fashioned in scheme. But it is old-fashioned only in the sense in which a classic is old-fashioned. Partly by reason of the skill with which the scheme is treated — that perfect technique which comes to other men through innumerable experiments, but came all unearned to Oscar Wilde — and much more by reason of the dialogue itself, which is incomparable in the musical elegance and swiftness of its wit, *Lady Windermere's Fan* is a classic assuredly. As time goes on, those artificialities of incident and characterization (irritating to us now, because we are in point of time so near to this play that we cannot discount them) will have ceased to matter. Our posterity will merely admire the deftness of the construction. And no lapse of time will dim the lustre of that wit which won for the play so much enthusiasm last Saturday. . . .

Max Beerbohm, *Saturday Review*,
reprinted in *Last Theatres*, p. 102-4

It is impossible . . . to read the letters which during the rehearsals passed between the author and the manager — very feudal and lordly letters from Wilde and purely practical ones from Alexander — without realizing that it was the manager at this time who was the more conscious of the two of the creaking conventions, the clever twists, the impossible transitions of character which were making the drama of the day a byword; who was the more anxious of the two to discard them. . . .

Alexander . . . wanted the [second] act to end not upon a tirade by the leading lady but upon a humorous and apposite comment by the man. . . .

Alexander . . . replied: 'The end of the second act is now better, but it could be better still and you could make it so if you took the trouble. I have pointed this out to you at almost every rehearsal but you only received my suggestion with contempt.'

A. E. W. Mason,
Sir George Alexander and the St. James Theatre, p. 33-6

Wilde, luckily, learnt sense, but he was reluctant to learn it when he began to rehearse his first comedy. He refused to listen to Alexander, who told him that it was a fundamental mistake to conceal the knowledge of Mrs. Erlynne's relationship to Lady Windermere until the last act, and it was not until the fact forced itself upon him after the first performance that he consented to make the revelation in the second act. . . .

For about a quarter of an hour, the five men converse in epigrams. This is the best part of the play, containing some of Wilde's wittiest remarks. . . . It has dramatic value at this point, for it provides a quiet time between the bouts of 'tornado'.

St. John Ervine, *Oscar Wilde*, p. 179, 213

In three sequences dense with thought Wilde shows his understanding of his characters' psychology, while keeping an ironic focus on the imperfections of society which make them behave as they do.

As above, p. 79-80

Mrs. Erlynne . . . as well as her daughter, has had something to learn and she has learnt. We feel the terrible weight of her realization: it gives added poignancy to her entreaty to Lady Windermere to keep silent about what really happened in Lord Darlington's rooms. . . . The audience must surely pick up here an oblique allusion to a searing moment in her dialogue with Lord Windermere, when he taunted her with what happened to her after she left her child: 'You abandoned her for your lover, who abandoned you in turn.' Wilde is calling in fact for close readings of the kind for which he is not usually given credit. Under the brittle snap of the dialogue the subterranean life of feeling is delicately conveyed.

As above, p. 82-3

How does this 'Story of a Good Woman' . . . strike us to-day? Though I could not have believed it thirty years ago, most favourably. . . . The plays of Oscar Wilde now seem as far from the realities of social life as Restoration comedy. They are, of course, extremely sentimental at their serious moments, but this sentiment now 'dates' so completely that it amuses without irritating. . . . It is unnecessary to worry ourselves about psychological improbabilities. The stagecraft is masterly. . . .

On the whole, the play went very well, and Mr. Cecil Beaton's three sets for it and his costumes were splendid and delightful.

Desmond MacCarthy, *New Statesman*, 1 Sept. 1945

John [Gielgud] was not an interfering producer . . . . I had had a great deal of experience in Restoration comedy, and I just got on with it. . . . A double staircase, with a bridge across, dominated the stage in the ball scene and we made great use of that feature. . . .

Athene Seyler, in conversation with Margery Morgan

Lady Windermere's Fan is a delight, and not simply for the pleasures, though these can hardly be overstated, of seeing Coral Browne as the Scarlet Lady, Wilfred Hyde White as her ineffably complaisant dupe, and Isabel Jeans as the Duchess of Berwick, past mistress in the exquisitely refined art of the bully. Also for sheer pleasure in the play itself. Anthony Quayle's production and Cecil Beaton's designs — dingy silk dresses, bulging with puffs and pads in all the colours of a fleshy, well-ripened bruise — strike precisely the note of Wilde's glamorous, worldly, tarnished and materialistic society.

Hilary Spurling, *The Spectator*, 21 Oct. 1966

A Woman of No Importance

A drama in four acts.
Written: 1892, under the original title *Mrs. Arbuthnot*.
First production: Haymarket Th., 19 April 1895 (prod. Herbert Beerbohm Tree who played Lord Illingworth, with Mrs. Bernard Beere as Mrs. Arbuthnot).
First American production: Fifth Avenue Th., New York, 11 Dec. 1895 (Rose Coghlan's company; planned tour cancelled on news of Wilde's arrest, in 1895).
Revived: in German, Neues Theater, Berlin, 4 Sept. 1903 (dir. Max Reinhardt); Haymarket Th., 1907, 1909 (with H. Beerbohm Tree); Kingsway Th., 13 May 1915 (Liverpool Repertory Th. Common-

wealth Company, dir. Madge McIntosh, who played Mrs. Arbuthnot); Fulton Th., New York, 24 Apr. 1916; Savoy Th., 12 Feb. 1953 (dir. Michael Benthall, des. Loudon Sainthill, with Athene Seyler as Lady Hunstanton, Isabel Jeans as Lady Allonby, Clive Brook as Lord Illingworth, Peter Barkworth as Gerald Arbuthnot); Congress Th., Eastbourne, 9 Oct.1967, trans. Vaudeville Th., 28 Nov. 1967 (adapted Paul Dehn, dir. Malcolm Farquhar, des. Jessica Gwynne, costumes William J. Winn, with Tony Britton as Lord Illingworth, Phyllis Calvert as Mrs. Arbuthnot, Agnes Lauchlan as Lady Hunstanton, Pauline Jameson as Mrs. Allonby, Michael Pennington as Gerald Arbuthnot); Th. Royal, Bury St. Edmunds, May 1988 (Cambridge Theatre Company, touring, dir. Bill Pryde, des. Kenny Miller).

First published: London: John Lane, 1894.

Most authoritative text: in *Two Society Comedies*, New Mermaid edition, 1982. In *Complete Plays*, Methuen, p. 301-77.

The theme of the differences between men and women, and especially the double standard of sexual morality, unites this play across a violent contrast of styles — the wittily ironic and the sentimentally melodramatic. Even more than usual in Wilde, the characters arouse ambiguous responses. The first three acts are set at Hunstanton Chase, where the dangerous Lord Illingworth and Mrs. Allonby fulfil the roles of the Valmont and Mme. de Meurteuil of their society. Awkwardly out-of-place in this sophisticated, aristocratic milieu are the young American 'puritan', Hester Worsley, and the poor bank clerk, Gerald Arbuthnot, to whom Illingworth has offered the post of secretary. Mrs. Allonby challenges Illingworth to kiss 'the puritan', but Act I ends when the handwriting on an envelope reminds him of a 'woman of no importance' he once knew. In Act II, Gerald's mother appears and is introduced by him to Illingworth: the 'victim' and her former seducer recognize each other, and Illingworth realizes, with pleasure, that Gerald is his son. Mrs. Arbuthnot is forced to accept that she can give Gerald no reason for her objections to his new appointment without exposing herself to his scorn. In Act III, Lord Illingworth's Schopenhauerian judgement against women is capped by Hester's implacable condemnation of those who have sinned against morality. Illingworth's off-stage kissing of Hester provokes Gerald's rage — and Mrs. Arbuthnot's revelation that he is

*about to strike his father. Act IV, in her own sitting-room, shows
Mrs. Arbuthnot refusing first Gerald's, then Illingworth's own
attempts to marry her to the father of her son. Gerald is to marry
the wealthy Hester. They and his mother, reconciled in love, can
do without a 'man of no importance'.*

We will devise schemes and undermine the foolish Tree, who must
engage you for my play.

It is absurd that I can't have the boy I want in the part, and there is no
one but you. The other young men are dreadful: you are an artist . . . .

You know you are my ideal Gerald, as you are my ideal friend.

> Wilde, to Sydney Barraclough, Dec. 1892 (two letters),
> in *Letters*, p. 324 (Fred Terry eventually played Gerald)

In my new play there are very few women's parts — it is a woman's
play — and I am of course limited to some degree to the stock company
at the Haymarket.

> Wilde, to Oswald Yorke, late Feb. 1893,
> in *Letters*, p. 335

There are some cuts to be made, and I don't know if the Americans, a
sensitive, over-sensitive people, will be annoyed at some foolish, good-
natured badinage about their country in the second act. If so, . . . we
could cut there: the lines are merely light comedy lines of no particular
value, except to Lord Illingworth.

> Wilde, to his American agent, Elizabeth Marbury,
> Feb. 1893, in *More Letters*, p. 119

With regard to the parts: Lady Stutfield is very serious and romantic —
she must play as if she was playing the heroine of a romance. Lady
Hunstanton is genial, loveable, and kind: Lady Caroline hard and bitter:
the girl simple and direct: the boy must be charming and young: as for
the mother, Agnes Booth must play it. Lord Illingworth requires great
distinction; the finest touch and style.

> Wilde, to Elisabeth Marbury, Feb. 1893, in *More Letters*, p. 120

The Company I saw at Jersey was, on the whole, very good. The Hester
Worsley wants decision, and strength. She is not strong enough in Act
IV, but she is very pretty and sweet.

> Wilde, to H. H. Morell, Sept. 1893
> (after seeing Tree's second touring company), in *Letters*, p. 345

Oscar and I went one morning for a walk, and he told me the plot of *The* [*sic*] *Woman of No Importance*. He had a beautiful voice — cultivated, melodious; and it was a rare treat to hear him as a raconteur. One of the guests told me that Oscar had read the last act to them one afternoon, and they had all been moved to tears, when Oscar, in his most impressive manner, said: 'I took that situation from *The Family Herald* !'

It was where 'The Woman of No Importance' strikes Lord Illingworth in the face with her glove. He loved descending from the sublime to the ridiculous.

Louise Jopling, *Twenty Years of My Life* (1925),
reprinted in Mikhail, *Interviews and Recollections*, I, p. 205

It is not his wit, . . . and still less his knack of paradox-twisting, that makes me claim for him a place apart among living English dramatists. It is the keenness of his intellect, the individuality of his point of view, the excellence of his verbal style, and, above all, the genuinely dramatic quality of his inspirations. I do not hesitate to call the scene between Lord Illingworth and Mrs. Arbuthnot at the end of the second act of this play the most virile and intelligent . . . piece of English dramatic writing of our day. It is the work of a man who knows life, and knows how to transfer it to the stage. There is no situation-hunting, no posturing. The interest of the scene arises from emotion based upon thought, thought thrilled with emotion. There is nothing conventional in it, nothing insincere. In a word, it is a piece of adult art. True, it is by far the best scene in the play. . . . But there are many details of similar, though perhaps not equal, value scattered throughout. . . .

How different is the 'He is your father!' tableau at the end of Act III from the strong and simple conclusion of Act II — how different, and how inferior! It would be a just retribution if Mr. Wilde were presently to be confronted with this tableau in all the horrors of chromo-lithography, on every hoarding in London. . . . I see no reason why Mrs. Arbuthnot should not take a more common-sense view of the situation. . . . Perhaps Mr. Wilde would have us believe that she suffers from mild religious mania. . . . But she herself admits that she does not repent the 'sin' that has given her a son to love. Well then, what is all this melodrama about? . . .

William Archer, *The World*, 26 April 1893,
reprinted in Archer, *The Theatrical 'World' for 1893*,
and in Beckson, *Oscar Wilde: the Critical Heritage*, p. 145-6

The witty or grotesque persons who flit about the hero and heroine,

Lord Illingworth, Mrs. Allonby, Canon Daubeny, Lady Stutfield, and Mr. Kelvil, all, in fact, who can be characterized by a sentence or a paragraph, are real men and women; and the most immoral among them have enough of the morality of self-control and self-possession to be pleasant and inspiriting memories. There is something of heroism in being always master enough of oneself to be witty. . . . Lord Illingworth and Mrs. Allonby have self-control and intellect; and to have these things is to have wisdom, whether you obey it or not. . . . And yet one puts the book down with disappointment . . . it is not a work of art. . . . The reason is that the tragic and emotional people who are important to the story, Mrs. Arbuthnot, Gerald Arbuthnot, and Hester Worsley, are conventions of the stage. . . . He falls back upon the popular conventions, the spectres and shadows of the stage.

> W. B. Yeats, in *The Bookman*, March 1895, reprinted in
> Beckson, *Oscar Wilde: the Critical Heritage*, p. 162-3

Mr. Wilde allowed the psychological idea to work itself out almost unmolested, and the play was, in my opinion, by far the most truly dramatic of his plays.

> Max Beerbohm, *Saturday Review*, 8 Dec. 1900,
> reprinted in *More Theatres*, p. 334

It was rather amusing, as it was a complete mass of epigrams, with occasional whiffs of grotesque melodrama and drivelling sentiment. The queerest mixture! Mr. Tree is a wicked Lord, staying in a country house, who has made up his mind to bugger one of the other guests — a handsome young man of twenty. The handsome young man is delighted; when his mother enters, sees his Lordship and recognizes him as having copulated with her twenty years before, the result of which was — the handsome young man. . . . She then appeals to the handsome young man, who says, 'Dear me! What an abominable thing to do — to go and copulate without marrying!' . . . and then suddenly enters (from the garden) a young American millionairess, with whom (very properly) the handsome young man is in love. . . . It seems an odd plot, doesn't it? But it required all my penetration to find out that this was the plot, as you may imagine. Epigrams engulf it like the sea. Most of them were thoroughly rotten, and nearly all were said quite cynically to the gallery. Poor old Tree sits down with his back to the audience to talk to a brilliant lady, and swings round in his seat every time he delivers an epigram. . . .

> Lytton Strachey, letter to Duncan Grant on
> Tree's 1909 revival of the play, quoted in
> Michael Holroyd, *Lytton Strachey: the Unknown Years*
> (Heinemann, 1967), p. 319

The period of the play is 1893. It is improbable that obscure young bank clerks with morose mothers, even in these times, are accustomed to frequent such country houses as are left, or to associate on familiar terms with ambassadors actual or potential, but they certainly were not accustomed to do so in 1893; a fact which must have been well within Wilde's knowledge. . . . [Mrs. Arbuthnot's] psuedo-literary fudge leaves Illingworth unmoved, as, indeed, it would leave better men than him. . . . A dramatist who sets out to reveal life should reveal life and not fanciful fiction. It is his business to know his characters so well that he can answer any questions about them. . . . How, we wonder, did Rachel reply to Gerald when, in his childhood and in his youth, he enquired about his father? . . .

St. John Ervine, *Oscar Wilde*, p. 226-34

Wilde's plays are, apart from their wit, the purest fudge, put together without any kind of artistic conscience, and using all the stalest devices of the theatre. . . . Not all the wit in Mayfair can sweeten that little tract called *A Woman of No Importance*.

James Agate, *Oscar Wilde*, p. 7

Tennants have knocked it [*A Woman of No Importance*] into three acts, relieved of some of its painful absurdity, refurbished with some additional witticisms, sumptuously set and dressed by Loudon Sainthill, produced by Michael Benthall, and performed at a stately pace by a company of the first quality. . . . But so much trouble has been taken to avoid the melodramatic booby-traps and tripwires . . . that there is all too little energy left for vivacity in the high comic and witty passages which are the only possible justification for reviving the play. . . . Athene Seyler and Isabel Jeans are quite admirable as Lady Hunstanton and Mrs. Allonby, but the mood of the production is against them.

Iain Hamilton, *The Spectator*, 20 Feb. 1953

When Michael Benthall produced *A Woman of No Importance* he wisely treated it as a comedy instead of the drama which Wilde intended it to be. The melodramatic scenes were pruned in the script, and toned down in the production, so that the emphasis of the play was entirely on Wilde's wit.

Norman Marshall, *The Producer and the Play*
(London: MacDonald, 1957), p. 258

Presumably, Mr. Dehn's intention was to render what is, after all, fifth-rate Wilde suitable for a modern audience. On reading the original, with its great windy stretches of purple rhetoric, one longs for the corruscating saltiness of, say, *East Lynne*. . . . There is hardly anything wrong with the adaptation as such; but when faced with a ruin, one should either leave it alone or knock it down. To try and shore it up with bricks from more sightly buildings can only result in this case in a kind of Oscar Memorial far more grotesque than Epstein's.

Mr. Dehn's restorative hand is in evidence everywhere. He has reduced the number of settings by half, and the number of acts from four to three. Greatly to his credit, he has turned a minor character — the Archdeacon — into a comic creation of such gentle hilarity as to outfrock Canon Chasuble. . . . Not so successful is Mr. Dehn's master-plan: to prune ruthlessly the melodramatic excesses of the plot, and fill in the resultant gaps with so many epigrams that the play, as it now stands, might be retitled *The Most of Wilde*. Some of the epigrams are borrowed from other Wildean works: some are presumably Mr. Dehn's own invention. . . . But the pastiche is skilfully done; and my only grumble is that the play itself gets bogged down in an endless swamp of aphoristic chatter. Shaw got away with it because his talk-ins were about something; Mr. Dehn doesn't, because *his* dialogues are about every-thing. At least Oscar knew when to stop.

How strange it is that the urbane Wilde could have written such a curtain line as 'Stop, Gerald, stop! He is your own father!' And it is even stranger that Mr. Dehn should have retained it. The play is so hopelessly out of date by now. . . .

Hugh Leonard, *Plays and Players*, Feb. 1968

It is a 'woman's play' in sympathy with women. . . . Wilde's characters . . . are busily occupied in filling in the time, getting through the long spaces of an ordinary afternoon, creating a stage on which their existence will have more point, with the aid of wit and story-telling. At a deep level — which most of them do not consciously recognize (Lord Illingworth and Mrs. Allonby are the brilliant exceptions: W. B. Yeats observed that they had a kind of 'wisdom') — they are engaged in the existential process which Wilde believed was the purpose of life. Through the immensely long conversation piece of the first act they are revealing in their own way the patterns of their inner life.

Katharine Worth, *Oscar Wilde*, p. 99

The world of Illingworth, Mrs. Allonby, and even Lady Hunstanton, is a subtle one, far indeed, one might think, from the simple, lurid world of melodrama. . . . In this play Wilde is especially interested in the curious relationship between the two worlds.

As above, p. 99-100

Mrs. Allonby is the first in a new line of women characters, a female dandy, who uses her wit with aplomb and ruthlessness to make life more amusing for herself. That 'double standard' . . . is to her no more than an extra titillation in the sexual game. . . . The long-drawn-out, frivolous dialogue among the women builds up an impression of a bold self-willed mental life only just below the surface of the decorous front the ladies present to the world.

As above, p. 102

By a radical change of context which placed the agonized woman in a more refined *intellectual* environment, Wilde made his audience see the traumatic situation as he had always seen it — as a quite unnecessary form of suffering.

Of course Mrs. Arbuthnot cannot see it this way. She, poor woman, is trapped in her time, not free of it, as Wilde was.

As above, p. 115

Cambridge Theatre Company handles this early Wilde play with such sympathy and style that the piece's rare appearance . . . is hard to understand until the last act, when the melodramatic plot that has been chugging along under epigrams steams into the open. . . . When Wilde's melodramatic slip starts showing . . . the audience . . . feels uncertain. Which is why *Lady Windermere's Fan* and *An Ideal Husband*, lesser plays on most counts but homogeneous in style, have generally been preferred.

Jeremy Kingston, *The Times*, 13 May 1988

An Ideal Husband

A play in four acts.
Written: 1893-94.
First production: Haymarket Th., 3 Jan. 1895 (with Lewis Waller as Sir Robert Chiltern, Charles Hawtrey as Lord Goring, Florence West as Mrs. Cheveley, Fanny Brough as Lady Markby, Julia Neilson as Lady Chiltern).

Revived: St. James's Th., 14 May 1914 (with George Alexander as Goring); Westminster Th., 16 Nov. 1943 (presented by Robert Donat, dir. Jack Minster, des. Rex Whistler, with Esmé Percy as Earl of Caversham, Roland Culver as Lord Goring, Irene Vanbrugh as Lady Markby, Manning Wiley as Sir Robert Chiltern, Martita Hunt as Mrs. Cheveley); Opera House, Manchester, 13 Oct. 1965, trans. Strand Th., London, 16 Dec. 1965 (dir. James Roose-Evans, des. Anthony Holland, with Roger Livesey as Earl of Caversham, Michael Denison as Sir Robert Chiltern, Dulcie Gray as Lady Chiltern, Ursula Jeans as Lady Markby, Margaret Lockwood as Mrs. Cheveley, Richard Todd as Lord Goring, Perlita Nielson as Mabel); Greenwich Th., 2 Feb. 1978 (dir. Robert Kidd); Chichester Festival Th., 13 May 1987 (dir. Tony Britton, des. Peter Rice, with Joanna Lumley as Mrs. Cheveley, Clive Francis as Goring); Westminster Th., 24 Apr. 1989 and on tour (dir. Patrick Sandford, des. Juliet Shillingford, with Jeremy Sinden as Lord Goring, Richard Murdoch as Earl of Caversham, Moira Redmond as Lady Markby, Jeremy Child as Sir Robert Chiltern, Liz Bagley as Lady Chiltern, Delia Lindsay as Mrs. Cheveley).

First published: as 'by the Author of *Lady Windermere's Fan*', London: Leonard Smithers, 1899. *Most authoritative text:* in *Two Society Comedies*, New Mermaid edition, 1983. In *Complete Plays*, Methuen, p. 105-212.

Film: British Lion/London Films, 1947 (dir. Alexander Korda, script Lagos Biro, costumes des. Cecil Beaton, with C. Aubrey Smith as Caversham, Hugh Williams as Sir Robert Chiltern, Michael Wilding as Goring, Diana Wynyard as Lady Chiltern, Paulette Goddard as Mrs. Cheveley, Constance Collier as Lady Markby, Glynis Johns as Mabel).

Wilde sets up an instructive contrast between Lord Goring, the witty, vain, but good-hearted raisonneur of this well-made play, a dandy who revels in the trivial, and the earnest, generally admired, rising statesman, Sir Robert Chiltern. During a reception at his splendid house, Sir Robert, who is idolized by his unworldly wife, is put under pressure by the sophisticated Mrs. Cheveley from Vienna, a femme fatale *who holds the secret of the corrupt deal on which his brilliant career was based. She wants him to repeat his previous treachery in variant form by advocating, in parliament, a dubious scheme to finance an Argentine canal. Mrs. Chevely is contrasted with the innocent*

*Lady Chiltern (they were school-fellows) and also with the
effervescent, irreverent Mabel, Chiltern's younger sister, who is
eventually happily matched with Lord Goring. Her claim to
have more in common with Sir Robert than has his wife has
evident force. Lord Goring intervenes to trap her by means of a
bracelet-brooch he once gave to a cousin, from whom Mrs.
Cheveley stole it; but she is ultimately defeated by Sir Robert's
unstrained confidence in his wife's love and loyalty. The
politician and his marriage are saved, and his wife accepts that
he can only fulfil his nature in public life by taking up the
Cabinet post he is offered. Yet the audience is left uncertain of
Chiltern's capacity for self-knowledge, and aware that this is a
character who must battle continually for moral integrity. This
is Wilde's most considerable reflection on the relation between
private and political morality.*

If Robert Chiltern, the Ideal Husband, were a common clerk, the
humanity of his tragedy would be none the less poignant. I have placed
him in the higher ranks of life merely because that is the side of social
life with which I am best accquainted.

> Wilde, in interview, *St. James's Gazette*, 18 Jan. 1895,
> reprinted in *Interviews and Recollections*, p. 196

The modern note is struck in Sir Robert Chiltern's assertion of the
individuality and courage of his wrongdoing as against the mechanical
idealism of his stupidly good wife, and in his bitter criticism of a love
that is only the reward of merit. It is from the philosophy on which this
scene is based that the most pregnant epigrams in the play have been
condensed. . . . In contriving the stage expedients by which the action of
the piece is kept going, Mr. Wilde has been once or twice a little too
careless of stage illusion: for example, why on earth should Mrs.
Chevely, hiding in Lord Goring's room, knock down a chair? . . .

> George Bernard Shaw, *Saturday Review*, 12 Jan. 1895,
> reprinted in *Our Theatres in the Nineties*, I, p. 10-12

The question which Mr. Wilde propounds is, 'Ought [Sir Robert
Chiltern's] old peccadillo to incapacitate him for public life?' — and,
while essaying to answer it in the negative, he virtually, to my thinking,
answers it in the affirmative. . . . It may be a mistake to hold a man

disabled by his past from doing service to the state; but this man is disabled by his present. The excellent Sir Robert proves himself one of those gentlemen who can be honest so long as it is absolutely convenient, and no longer. . . . *An Ideal Husband* is a very able and entertaining piece of work, charmingly written, wherever Mr. Wilde can find it in his heart to sufflaminate his wit. . . .

> William Archer, *Pall Mall Budget*, 10 Jan. 1895,
> reprinted in *The Theatrical 'World' of 1895*

The reader should remember that the time of the play is 1895, in which year Chiltern is forty. He was, therefore, twenty when the Suez Canal shares were bought. . . . It is unlikely that he would, at twenty, have been private secretary to a prominent politician. . . . *An Ideal Husband* is not intended to be a common-place, back-street melodrama for unexacting people: it is high comedy, reflecting life, and is designed for the entertainment of intelligent and informed people. . . . High comedy should not outrage the understanding . . .

> St. John Ervine, *Oscar Wilde*, p. 261-5

Modern research suggests that Frank Harris offered Wilde the plot, and that Wilde jumped at the offer. I can well believe that this was so; I should have much greater difficulty in thinking that this wittiest of playwrights took the slightest interest in what emotions Lord X. was feeling between paradoxes, or what Lady Y. was meditating between *bêtises*.

> James Agate, *Oscar Wilde*, p. 8

The present production of *An Ideal Husband*, directed by Jack Minster, rivals John Gielgud's production of *Love for Love*. The scenery and costumes designed by Rex Whistler are a delight to the eye, and the acting is of a high order throughout. . . . It is interesting to discover that on the stage this play of Wilde's is as witty and amusing as ever, but also at the present moment it brings back such an air of civilization and refreshment. . . . To point out the defects in an artificial comedy so brilliant as this is like criticizing a box of first-rate crystallized fruits, you either delight in them or you do not.

> James Redfern, *The Spectator*, 26 Nov. 1943

The high comedy of it is splendid . . . but its purpose is no more than to obscure the incredible foolishness of what is no more than third-rate melodrama.... The play continues elegantly to amuse in Tony Britton's riplingly deft and stylish production, equipped with three sumptuous-looking sets by Peter Rice and performances that are good where it matters.

Kenneth Hurren, *Plays and Players*, July 1987

Wilde both exploits and sends up the conventions of Victorian melodrama. You can make that reassuring observation from the haven of the end of Act IV when the curtain has come down on this revival. At the end of Act II, however, we are not so sure....

Christopher Edwards, *The Spectator*, 29 Mar. 1989

Jeremy Sinden takes the best part as Lord Goring....Trying to look like Oscar Wilde in his prime, he more resembles Nigel Lawson.... This is an elegant and sinister show, as relevant to modern politics as it is to Wilde's downfall.

D. A. N. Jones, *Sunday Telegraph*, 30 Apr. 1989

A thinly disguised vein of mysogyny runs through the piece like a fault in character not detected at the time.

Sylvester Onwordi, *What's On*, 3 May 1989

The Importance of Being Earnest

A comedy in three or four acts.

Written: in four acts, Aug. and Sept. 1894; one scene cut, the rest condensed into three acts, at George Alexander's request, for 1895 production. The provisional title was *Lady Lancing*.

First production: St. James's Th., 14 Feb. 1895 (prod. George Alexander, who also played John Worthing, with Allan Aynesworth as Algernon, Rose Leclerq as Lady Bracknell, Irene Vanburgh as Gwendolen, Evelyn Millard as Cecily); rev. 26 June 1911, 7 March 1913.

First production in German: as *Bunbury*, Kleines Theater, Berlin, 22 Feb. 1902, private matinee (dir. Max Reinhardt).

Revived: Haymarket Th., 21 Nov. 1923 (dir. Allan Aynesworth, with Margaret Scudamore, Leslie Faber, and Louise Hampton); Lyric Th., Hammersmith, 7 July 1930 (dir. Nigel Playfair, des. Michael Weight, with Mabel Terry-Lewis and John Gielgud); Old Vic Th., 5 Feb. 1934 (dir. Tyrone Guthrie, with Roger Livesey as John Worthing, Athene Seyler as Lady Bracknell, Flora Robson as Gwendolen, Ursula Jeans as Cecily, Elsa Lanchester as Miss Prism, Charles Laughton as Canon Chasuble, James Mason as Merriman); Globe Th., 31 Jan. 1939 (dir. John Gielgud, who also played John Worthing, des. Motley, with Edith Evans as Lady Bracknell, Margaret Rutherford as Miss Prism, Angela Baddeley as Cecily, Joyce Carey as Gwendolen, Ronald Ward as Algernon, Leon Quartermaine as Lane); Globe Th., 16 Aug. 1939 (dir. John Gielgud, who also played John Worthing, with Edith Evans, Margaret Rutherford, Peggy Ashcroft as Cecily, Gwen Ffrangcon-Davies as Gwendolen, Jack Hawkins as Algernon), toured after outbreak of war, re-opening Globe Th., 26 Dec. 1939, revived Phoenix Th., 14 Oct. 1942 (dir. John Gielgud, cast as before except that Cyril Ritchard appeared as Algernon, Jean Cadell as Miss Prism, J. H. Roberts as Chasuble); Old Vic Th., 13 Oct. 1959 (dir. Michael Benthall, music by John Lambert, des. Desmond Heeley, with John Justin as John Worthing, Alec McCowen as Algernon, Fay Compton as Lady Bracknell, Judi Dench as Cecily, Barbara Jefford as Gwendolen, Miles Malleson as Chasuble); Ashcroft Th., Croydon, 29 March 1965 (dir. Toby Robertson, with Neil Stacey as John Worthing, Roy Marsden as Algernon, Marian Spencer as Lady Bracknell, Sylvia Coleridge as Miss Prism); Th. Royal, Brighton, 23 Jan. 1968, trans Haymarket Th., 8 Feb 1968 (dir. Robert Chetwynd, des. Michael Annals, with Daniel Massey as John Worthing, John Standing as Algernon, Isabel Jeans as Miss Prism, Robert Eddison as Chasuble); Shaw Th., 8 March 1974 (dir. Peter James, des. Bernard Culshaw, with Betty Marsden as Lady Bracknell, Polly Adams as Gwendolen); Greenwich Th., 20 March 1975 (dir. Jonathan Miller, des. Patrick Robertson, costumes Rosemary Vercoe, with Irene Handl as Lady Bracknell, David Horowitz as Jack Worthing, Robert Swann as Algernon, Angela Down as Gwendolen, Charlotte Cornwell as Cecily, Benjamin Whitrow as Chasuble); Avon Stage, Stratford, Ontario, 10 June 1976 (dir. Robin Phillips, des. Daphne Dare and Molly Harris Campbell, with Nicholas Pennell as John Worthing, William Hutt as Lady Bracknell); Round House, 15 Dec. 1977 (Actors' Company, dir. Tenniel Evans, who also played Lane and Merriman, des. Stephanie Howard, with Edward Petherbridge as Chasuble); Young Vic. Th., 22 Dec. 1977 (dir. Denise Coffey, des. Robert Dein, costumes Alix Stone, with Teddy Green as Lady Bracknell, Amanda Boxer as Gwendolen, Natasha Pyne as Cecily); National Th. at Lyttelton Th., 16 Sept. 1982 (dir. Peter Hall, des. John Bury, with Judi Dench as Lady Bracknell, Martin Jarvis as John Worthing, Nigel Havers as Algernon, Anna

Massey as Miss Prism, Paul Rogers as Chasuble); Royalty Th.,
7 Sept. 1987 (dir. Donald Sinden, des. Carl Toms, with Wendy Hiller
and Clive Francis); Bloomsbury Th., 16 May 1989, as part of tour
(Talawa Company, dir. Yvonne Brewster).

First production of four-act version: Wanstead Players, Jan. 1955;
revived: A.D.C. Theatre, Cambridge, 11 March 1958.

First published: three-act version, as 'by the Author of *The Importance
of Being Earnest*', London: Leonard Smithers, 1899; four-act version,
ed. S. A. Dickson, 1956.

Most authoritative text: New Mermaid edition, 1980. Three-act version
in *Complete Plays*, Methuen, p. 213-92, and text from four-act
version as appendix, p. 293-9.

Musical version: as *Half in Earnest*, by Vivian Ellis, opened the
Belgrade Th., Coventry, 27 March 1958.

Film: Rank/Javelin/Two Cities, 1952 (dir. and script Anthony Asquith,
with Michael Redgrave as John Worthing, Michael Denison as
Algernon, Edith Evans as Lady Bracknell, Margaret Rutherford as
Miss Prism, Joan Greenwood as Gwendolen, Dorothy Tutin as
Cecily, Miles Malleson as Chasuble. 'As a record of a theatrical
performance . . . it is valuable' — Halliwell's *Film Guide*.)

Wilde travesties a universal plot — used by Euripides in Ion *and
in Shakespeare's late romances — concerned with the discovery
of true identities and the consequent reconciliation of the long-
separated members of a family. He makes this the vehicle for a
satire on contemporary society: its class structure, its worship
of money, its use of manners and conventions, dictated by
women, to inhibit freedom and joy and maintain the pattern of
dominance. Wilde uses coincidence and improbability to create
a fantasy version of life: farce translated into the style of high
comedy. In seeking the redoubtable Lady Bracknell's consent
for his engagement to her daughter Gwendolen, John Worthing
reveals that he was a foundling. She dismisses his appeal and
advises him that it is vital he should find an identity. Jack and
his friend Algernon (Lady Bracknell's nephew) have both
exercised their powers of invention to evade some of the
pressures of society: as alibis, Jack has invented a scapegrace
brother called Ernest, and Algernon an invalid friend named
Bunbury. Algernon's discovery of Jack's double life sets him
on the track of Jack's young ward Cecily. He makes her
acquaintance by visiting Jack's house in the country, claiming*

to be Ernest. *Both men's pretences are exposed when Jack arrives in mourning for Ernest; whereupon, the insistence of both Cecily and Gwendolen that they will only marry a man called Ernest sets both men arranging a rebirth (through christening) in that name and image. The necessity for this is obviated by the revelations of Miss Prism, Cecily's governess, recognized by Lady Bracknell as a nursemaid who once mislaid a baby. So it is discovered that Jack is Algy's brother, and that their father's name was Ernest. The play is set for a triple (ironic) happy ending — for Miss Prism and Canon Chasuble as well as the two younger couples. So established values (Lady Bracknell's) are preserved — yet they are also annihilated by the 'butterfly' mood and style. In the scene which was cut from the original production and not published for many years, Algy, claiming to be Ernest, is faced by a solicitor with the prospect of imprisonment for debts run up by Jack under his alias. Cecily persuades Jack to pay up and thus save 'Ernest'.*

[I] am just finishing a new play which, as it is quite nonsensical and has no serious interest, will I hope bring me in a lot of red gold.

Wilde, to C. S. Mason, Aug. 1894, *Letters*, p. 364

As you wished to see my somewhat farcical comedy, I send you the first copy of it. It is called *Lady Lancing* on the cover: but the real title is *The Importance of Being Earnest*. When you read the play, you will see the punning title's meaning. Of course, the play is not suitable to you at all: you are a romantic actor: the people it wants are actors like Wyndham and Hawtrey.

Wilde, to George Alexander, *c.* 25 Oct. 1894, *Letters*, p. 376.

I hope you will enjoy my 'trivial' play. It is written by a butterfly for butterflies.

Wilde, to Arthur L. Humphreys, *Letters*, p. 382

It is exquisitely trivial, a delicate bubble of fancy, and it has its philosophy. . . . That we should treat all the trivial things of life very seriously, and all the serious things of life with sincere and studied triviality.

Wilde, interview in *St. James's Gazette*, 18 Jan. 1895, reprinted in *Interviews and Recollections*, p. 195

Oscar Wilde may be said to have at last, and by a single stroke, put his enemies under his feet. Their name is legion, but the most inveterate of them may be defied to go to St. James's Theatre and keep a straight face through the performance of *The Importance of Being Earnest*. It is a pure farce of Gilbertian parentage, but loaded with drolleries, epigrams, impertinences, and bubbling comicalities that only an Irishman could have ingrafted on that respectable Saxon stock. Since *Charley's Aunt* was first brought from the provinces to London I have not heard such unrestrained, incessant laughter from all parts of the theatre, and those laughed the loudest whose approved mission it is to read Oscar long lectures in the press on his dramatic and ethical shortcomings. The thing is as slight in structure and as devoid of purpose as a paper balloon, but it is extraordinarily funny, and the universal assumption is that it will remain on the boards here for an indefinitely extended period.

> H[amilton] F[yfe], *New York Times*, 17 Feb. 1895;
> reprinted in *Critical Heritage*, p. 188-9

I cannot say that I greatly cared for *The Importance of Being Earnest*. It amused me, of course; but unless comedy touches me as well as amuses me, it leaves me with a sense of having wasted my evening. I go to the theatre to be moved to laughter, not to be tickled or bustled into it; and that is why, though I laugh as much as anybody at a farcical comedy, I am out of spirits before the end of the second act, and out of temper before the end of the third, my miserable mechanical laughter intensifying these symptoms at every outburst. If the public ever becomes intelligent enough to know when it is really enjoying itself and when it is not, there will be an end of farcical comedy. Now in *The Importance of Being Earnest* there is plenty of this rib-tickling: for instance, the lies, the deceptions, the cross purposes, the sham mourning, the christening of the two grown-up men, the muffin eating, and so forth. These could only have been raised from the farcical plane by making them occur to characters who had, like Don Quixote, convinced us of their reality and obtained some hold on our sympathy. . . . On the whole I must decline to accept *The Importance of Being Earnest* as a day less than ten years old; and I am altogether unable to perceive any uncommon excellence in its presentations.

> G.B.S., *Saturday Review*, 23 Feb. 1895;
> reprinted in *Our Theatres in the Nineties, II*, 1932, p. 41-4

Paradoxical as it may sound in the case of so merry and light-hearted a play, *The Importance of Being Earnest* is artistically the most serious work that Wilde produced for the theatre. . . . With all its absurdity, its psychology is truer, its criticism of life subtler and more profound, than that of the other plays. And even in its technique it shows, in certain details, a breaking away from the conventional well-made play of the 'seventies and 'eighties in favour of the looser construction and more naturalistic methods of the newer school. . . .

In *The Importance of Being Earnest* . . . Wilde really invented a new type of play, and that type was the only quite original thing he contributed to the English stage. In form it is farce, but in spirit and in treatment it is comedy. Yet it is not farcical comedy. . . . There are only two other plays which I can think of which belong to the same type — [Shaw's] *Arms and the Man* and *The Philanderer*. *Arms and the Man*, like *The Importance of Being Earnest*, is psychological farce, a farce of ideas. . . . But *The Importance of Being Earnest* is only a joke, though an amazingly brilliant one, and Wilde seems to have looked upon it with the same amused contempt with which he looked on its predecessors. Perhaps he did not realize how good it was. At least he treated it with scant respect, for the original script was in four acts, and these were boiled down into three and the loose ends joined up in perfunctory fashion for purposes of representation. . . .

St. John Hankin, *Fortnightly Review*, May 1908

The Importance of Being Earnest has been revived by Mr. Alexander at the St James's Theatre, and is as fresh and as irresistible as ever. . . . Of the plays that he wrote specifically for production in London theatres, it is the finest, the most inalienably his own. In *Lady Windermere's Fan* and *A Woman of No Importance* and *An Ideal Husband*, you are aware of the mechanism — aware of Sardou. In all of them there is, of course, plenty of humanity, and of intellectual force, as well as of wit and humour; and these qualities are the more apparent for the very reason that they are never fused with the dramatic scheme, which was a thing alien and ready-made. . . . Not even in this play had Oscar Wilde invented a form of his own. On the contrary, the bare scenario is of the tritest fashion in the farce-writing of the period. . . . This very ordinary clod the magician picked up, turning it over in his hands — and presto! a dazzling prism for us. . . . Part of the play's fun, doubtless, is in the unerring sense of beauty that informs the actual writing of it. The absurdity of the situation is made doubly absurd by the contrasted grace and dignity of everyone's utterance. The play abounds, too, in perfectly chiselled apothegms — witticisms unrelated to action or character, but so good in themselves as to have the quality of dramatic surprise. . . . But, of course, what keeps the play so amazingly fresh is not the inlaid wit, but the humour, the ever-fanciful and inventive humour, irradiating every scene. Out of a really funny situation Oscar Wilde would get dramatically the last drop of fun, and then would get as much fun again out of the correlative notions aroused in him by that situation. . . . Imagine an ordinary dramatist's treatment of the great scene in the second act — the scene when Jack Worthing, attired in deepest mourning, comes to announce the death of the imaginary brother who is at this moment being impersonated on the premises by Algernon. . . . If the audience knew at the beginning of the act that Jack was presently to arrive in deep mourning, the fun would be well enough. On the other hand, if, when he arrived, it had to be explained to them why he was in deep mourning, and what was his mission, there would be no fun at all. But the audience is in neither of these states. In the first act, Jack has casually mentioned, once or twice, that he means to 'kill off' his imaginary brother. But he doesn't say when or how he is going to do it. As the second act opens and proceeds, the audience has forgotten all about his intention. They are preoccupied by Algernon. And so, when the sable figure of Jack at length appears, they are for a moment bewildered, and then they vaguely remember, and there is a ripple of laughter, and this ripple swells gradually to a storm of laughter, as the audience gradually realizes the situation in its full richness. None but a man with innate instinct for the theatre could have contrived this effect. But the point is that only Oscar Wilde, having contrived the effect, could have made the subsequent scene a worthy pendant to it. . . .

> Max Beerbohm, *Saturday Review*, 11 Dec. 1909,
> reprinted in *Last Theatres*, p. 508-11

The frowsy first act scenery . . . gave the impression that Algernon lived in a museum. . . .

The revival was more than saved by Miss Athene Seyler, Miss Flora Robson, and Miss Ursula Jeans. As Lady Bracknell Miss Seyler, who normally looks like some magnanimous mouse, swelled to Wagnerian size and gave a performance of such bite and gusto that every line was in danger of . . . being drowned in the laughter greeting the one before. But Miss Seyler knows what she is about, and did not throw away a comma.

> James Agate, on 1934 production at Old Vic,
> reprinted in *First Nights*, p. 284

The Importance was not a wise choice. Nobody was really well suited. My direction was galumphing and uninteresting. The revival must be unique in that Canon Chasuble (Charles Laughton in a devastating, brilliant, and outrageous lampoon) appeared to be the leading part. Business was good, but all memories of the production fortunately suffered a total eclipse by John Gielgud's glittering revival a few years later . . . the high-water mark in the production of artificial comedy in our epoch.

Tyrone Guthrie, *A Life in the Theatre*
(London: Hamish Hamilton, 1961), p. 113-14

Charles Laughton created unpleasantness in the company. . . . Tyrone Guthrie had a way of making comments that were not helpful to actors. . . . Flora Robson, generally a tragic actress, not used to playing in comedy, showed her delight to her 'mother' in the play every time she got a laugh. . . .

Athene Seyler, in conversation with Margery Morgan

As John Worthing, John [Gielgud] won an immediate success [*at the Lyric, Hammersmith, in 1929*]. With his slim, straight back, his meticulous elegance and his air of nobility which he can tilt into a lordly languor, he has all the qualities for Wilde's mannered comedy. Adjusting the angle of his hat with arrogant affectation, shooting a cuff as if he were playing an ace, dabbing fastidiously at his crocodile tears with an immaculate black-edged handkerchief from his breast pocket . . . he conveyed the impression of being quite capable of inventing for himself the perfect lines the author had given him, and in *Earnest* he exploited again his characteristic combination of seriousness and sincerity. . . . But this time there was a subtle exaggeration of the basic qualities and a delicately measured self-consciousness which produced the ideal quotient of comic affectation.

Ronald Hayman, *John Gielgud* (London: Heinemann, 1971), p. 66

I know those kind of women. They ring the bell and ask you to put a lump of coal on. They were caricatures, those people — absolutely assured, arrogant, and that's the way they spoke. . . . They spoke meticulously, they were all very good looking and they didn't have any nerves. . . .

Edith Evans, on Lady Bracknell, quoted in Hayman, as above, p. 120

John's inventions [*for 1939 production*] included a bird which warbled through the garden scene, interrupting Gwendolen, a church clock which heralded John Worthing's entrance in mourning and chimed four as tea was punctually served, and a step-ladder to climb when looking for the Army Lists on a high bookshelf. . . . As at Hammersmith, he gave a subtle parody of his own seriousness in a tragic role. . . .

Ronald Hayman, as above, p. 121

The secret of performing artificial comedy is to impersonate people who are already impersonating themselves and revelling in acting their own characters. Every gesture and intonation should be self-deflating; never a betrayal of direct feeling. . . . Miss Edith Evans's Lady Bracknell is a masterpiece of controlled extravagance. The temptation to overdo that lady's portentousness is subtly resisted, and yet the crescendos of her absurdity are beautifully distinct. Miss Evans keeps still — that was important, as the smallest movement on Lady Bracknell's part conveys the full horror of her amazement and disapproval. . . .

Undoubtedly, this is the best revival of *The Importance of Being Earnest*. . . . The very end (which is the weak part) ought to be taken much faster. There is nothing to be done with it but hurry it through with reckless gaiety. . . . But what a care-destroying work and what a good performance!

Desmond MacCarthy,
New Statesman and Nation, 26 Aug. 1939

Nothing is easier than to handle this play without noticing what it contains. It is so consistently farcical in tone, characterization, and plot that very few care to root out any more serious content. The general conclusion has been that Wilde merely decorates a silly play with a flippant wit. . . .

Insensitivity to slight and delicate things is insensitivity *tout court*. That is what Wilde meant when he declared that the man who despises superficiality is himself superficial. His best play . . . is about . . . that kind of false seriousness which means priggishness, hypocrisy, and lack of irony. . . . Wilde is as much of a moralist as Bernard Shaw, but . . . instead of presenting the problems of modern society directly, he flits around them, teasing them. . . . His wit . . . is a flickering, a coruscation, intermittently revealing the upper class of England in a bizarre light. . . .

One does not find Wilde's satire embedded in plot and character as in traditional high comedy. It is a running accompaniment to the play, and this . . . is the making of a new sort of comedy. . . . Flippancies repeated, developed, and . . . elaborated almost into a system amount to something in the end. . . . His witticisms are in ironic counterpoint with the absurdities of the action. This counterpoint is Wilde's method. . . . It is what makes him hard to catch. . . .

Eric Bentley, *The Modern Theatre*, p. 120-4

The Importance of Being Earnest is [Wilde's] exuberant parody of the trivial comedies (his own amongst them) which the serious people had established in the English theatre. It contains all the features of Wilde's earlier plays — the shameful secret (Worthing's origin in a handbag), the mistaken and assumed identities (Bunburying), and the sensational dénouement in which Worthing turns out to be Lady Bracknell's long-lost nephew. It even contains a sally against the dual morality which distinguished between male and female infidelity. . . . In tone *The Importance of Being Earnest* also owes a good deal to W. S. Gilbert's exploitation of ludicrous logic, and for several incidents it borrows freely from his *Engaged*. Yet with all these debts the play remains triumphantly alive. . . . The frankly farcical characters and treatment of *Charley's Aunt* . . . make Wilde's achievement in keeping his balance all the finer.

George Rowell,
The Victorian Theatre, p. 111-12

W. H. Auden . . . saw the play as a coded confession, and might without undue fancy have gone further. When Algy says that 'a man who marries without knowing Bunbury has a very tedious time of it', he isn't speaking only for Wilde and the distinctively gay 'nineties. . . . Earnest equals Ernest; the inimitable algebra of Victorian hypocrisy.

Yet that subject is only glancingly visible beneath the artifice. Spotting it is like diagnosing something deep and intestinal inside someone wearing a surcoat of paste diamonds. And this creates quite a problem for a director. How much humanity can he inject into characters who, as Auden suggests, often seem the merest excuses for Wildean apophthegms? . . . It's usual to dismiss the poor notice Shaw originally gave the play as the result of deafness or even envy; but others, too, must have felt 'tickled or bustled' rather than 'moved' to laughter by a Wilde whose brilliance is often 'mechanical'.

Indeed I suspect the first-night audience at the National sometimes felt that way. Its laughter came in hiccoughs, with barren patches between them, and seemed to be at its heartiest when someone managed to live rather than dazzle. . . . It was, surely, no accident that the audience audibly perked up at the re-appearance of a Lady Bracknell who was being played in a markedly more 'real' way than usual.

Not that I was altogether enraptured with Judi Dench's performance, splendid actress though she is. While it's perfectly permissible to hint that Lady Bracknell is something of a social *arriviste*, it's surely presumptuous and distracting to imply that she's slightly in love with her nephew, Algy. . . . The lines Wilde gives Lady Bracknell convince me that she's much more senior than Miss Dench makes her. . . . The ringingly imperious rotundities the character must enunciate . . . are custom-built for the mouth of a majestic old monster, and on a younger tongue sound improbably overweight, like marble columns on a hearthrug. . . .

The relative carefulness of Peter Hall's production is evident from the very start. . . . And yet the problem remains. . . . How to integrate Wilde the virtuoso wit with the Wilde who, behind it all, saw, felt, and suffered?

Benedict Nightingale, *New Statesman*, 24 Sept. 1982

As well as being an existential farce, *The Importance of Being Earnest* is his supreme demolition of late nineteenth-century social and moral attitudes, the triumphal conclusion to his career as revolutionary moralist.

Katharine Worth, *Oscar Wilde*, p. 155

There is . . . a little germ of existential anxiety in the great joke: 'being' in an empty hand-bag; being in a void. Like a Vladimir or a Winnie in Beckett's empty spaces, Jack has to construct himself from virtually nothing.

Katharine Worth, as above, p. 165-6

Gribsby [*in the suppressed scene*] is both halves of Parker and Gribsby, a sort of Jekyll-and-Hyde firm of solicitors, answering to the former name on pleasant, to the latter on 'more serious' occasions. This detail [is] found in a manuscript version of Act II. . . .

Rodney Shewan, *Oscar Wilde: Art and Egotism*, p. 223

b: Incomplete Plays

A Florentine Tragedy

Fragment of a blank verse drama in one act.

Written: 1894. ('This play seems virtually finished,' judged Richard
    Ellmann. However, T. Sturge Moore wrote a new opening scene for
    the first English production.)

First production in German: Deutsches Theater, Berlin, 12 Jan. 1906
    (dir. Max Reinhardt, in programme of three short plays).

First English production: Literary Theatre Society, as curtain-raiser to
    Salomé, King's Hall, London, 10 June 1906 (dir. and des. Charles
    Ricketts).

First American production: Grove Street Th., New York, 1 Feb. 1927
    (Grand Guignol Players).

Revived: Edinburgh, 19 Sept. 1908 (with Mrs. Patrick Campbell as
    Bianca); Birmingham Repertory Th., 1914-15; Kingsway Th., 22 Feb.
    1921 (dir. Cyril Hardingham, who also played Bardi); Arts Th.,
    26 June 1927 (dir. A.E. Filmer, with Walter Hudd, Ion Swinley, and
    Dorothy Black); Davenport, USA, Feb. 1956.

First published: in Russian, Moscow, Jan. 1907; and in *Collected
    Works*, 1908, with T. Sturge Moore's first scene. In *Complete Plays*,
    Methuen, p. 579-96, without Sturge Moore's additional scene.

---

*The merchant, Simone, returns home to find his wife, Bianca,
entertaining Guido Bardi, a young lord of renaissance Florence.
He is suspicious of them, and they are contemptuous of him,
attitudes expressed in constant innuendo. Simone, the most
complex and interesting character, lavishes courtesy on Guido
until his trap closes on a proposal for a duel. Bianca eggs her
lover on to kill her husband. In the event, Simone is victorious,
and the fragment ends with a strange reconciliation between
husband and wife, based on a fresh recognition of each other's
natural qualities.*

I am going at Rouen to try to rewrite my *Love and Death — Florentine
Tragedy*.

Wilde, to Robert Ross, 4 Sept. 1897,
in *Letters*, p. 638

A Florentine Tragedy

A Florentine Tragedy (produced for the first time) is akin to *Salomé* as being an essay in the art of suspense. We know there must be at least one death before the curtain falls; and the elaborate decorations interposed do not make us forget it: they do but give us time to become uncomfortable. Nor are they, as in *Salomé*, a mere artistic device of the author. They come from the nature of the chief character devised. Simone, the Florentine merchant, is a man of grim humour; and so, when he surprises his wife in the company of a young nobleman, he does not instantly draw his sword. He is furious; but his fury he will be able to express later. Meanwhile he can have some fun. He can fool the couple to the top of their bent, then suddenly drop a hint that will make them start, then again soothe them into security till he choose to frighten them again. His vengeance will be all the sweeter, all the more terrible, for such dalliance. He plays on his young wife's contempt for him, cringing to the stranger, descanting unctuously on this or that ware that he would sell. His desire is not merely to humiliate her. If she does not love the stranger yet, she shall by force of contrast be made to love him. His death shall be a dagger through her own heart. At length, after he has taken his fill of pretence, he challenges the lover to fight. The lover, worsted, begs for mercy, and is allowed to go on begging before Simone, with more than necessary violence, despatches him. The wife shrinks against the wall. . . . And now comes the ending for the sake of which, I take it, the play was written — the germ of psychological paradox from which the story developed itself backwards. The wife falls to her knees, and, with real love in her voice, cries 'Why did you not tell me you were so strong?' The husband pauses, stares at her, lets drop his dagger, saying 'Why did you not tell me you were so beautiful?' . . . Is the paradox a sound one? I think so. It is not unnatural that the merchant, having won his bride with money, should not have appreciated her at her full human value until he had won her by more primitive, more human means. Her contempt for him, moreover, would have prejudiced him against her. The light of admiration for him in her eyes, besides making her actually more beautiful, would have quickened his perception of her beauty. And then there was the fact that she had inspired a passion in the nobleman. This, too, would have quickened the merchant's perception. My sole objection to the paradox is concerned with the placing of it. No play — no work of art whatsoever — ought to finish on a top note. We ought never to be left gasping, at the fall of the curtain. . . .

Obviously, the part of Simone is a fine part for an actor. I should like to have seen it played by Sir Henry Irving. I know of no one else who could have given fully the sardonic essence of it. Mr George Ingleton, however, who played it the other night, is a very capable actor; and his performance seemed really distinguished in the glare of incapacity shed by the young lady and gentleman who played the two other parts.

Max Beerbohm, *Last Theatres*, p. 249-51

It leaves an impression of poetry, although the famous phrase, 'a windy brawler in a whirl of words', comes a little too near literal truth. . . . Wilde's melancholy and bejewelled rhetoric in this little tragedy. . . . These early sixteenth century creatures of passion do often express themselves tragically, but their speech is too heavily ornamented to strike a balance with its simple dramatic content. It takes Mr. Ion Swinley, for instance, fully five minutes to strangle Mr. Walter Hudd for the simple reason that he is engaged in an envenomed, picturesque tirade against the deceitfulness of mankind. . . . We listen attentively to Simone, for Mr. Swinley has a fine voice and uses it with intelligence. . . . Still, drama of a kind is undoubtedly there, and the jealous merchant's misanthropy is as good and as sincere a theatrical effect as Wilde employed.

The Times, 27 June 1927

La Sainte Courtisane

Fragmentary one-act play.
Written: 1894. Original manuscript lost; published fragment reconstructed from leaves of a first draft.
No performance traced.
First published: in *Collected Works*, second edition, Methuen, 1909. In *Complete Plays*, Methuen, p. 597-606.

A Wife's Tragedy

Unfinished prose play.
Written: probably early to mid 1890s.
Unperformed and *unpublished* (manuscript draft is in Clark Memorial Library, University of California, Los Angeles).

c: Scenarios and Adaptations

The Cardinal of Avignon

Scenario.
Originally written: 1882; taken up again in 1884, when Richard
    Mansfield showed interest in it.
First published: in Mason, *Bibliography*, 1914, p. 583-5, where text is
    described as written in 1884. Wilde sent a 'Shelleyesque' scenario to
    George Alexander in 1894, but this may have been for a different
    play.

Mr. and Mrs. Daventry

A play in four acts by Frank Harris, based on a scenario by Oscar Wilde.
Written: scenario, 1894; play, *c*. 1900.
First production: Royalty Th., 25 Oct. 1900 (with Mrs. Patrick
    Campbell, Gerald du Maurier, and George Arliss).
First published: Richards Press, 1956, with introduction by
    H. Montgomery Hyde.
Scenario published: in *Letters*, p. 360-2.

'What do you think of this for a play for you? A man of rank and fashion
marries a simple sweet country girl — a lady — but simple and ignorant
of fashionable life. They live at his country place and after a time he gets
bored with her. . . .

'*I want the sheer passion of love to dominate everything*. No morbid
self sacrifice. No renunciation — a sheer flame of love between a man
and a woman. That is what the play is to rise to — from the social
chatter of Act I. . . .' The story and the characters which made it live
were Wilde's from the beginning to the end.

Hesketh Pearson, quoting Wilde to Alexander,
in *Oscar Wilde*, p. 89-90

If, as Mr. Sherard admits, Harris paid Wilde two sums of £50 each for
the plot of *Daventry*, he paid him £99 19s 10d too much. As to a single
line having been by Oscar, either Mr. Sherard does not know chalk from

cheese . . . or else he has never read a line of *Daventry* or seen it acted. If Oscar had written it, it would now be a classic.

Bernard Shaw, Preface to 1938 edition of
Frank Harris, *Oscar Wilde*, p. xxv

The Critic as Artist

By Charles Marowitz. The text of Wilde's essay in dialogue form was edited, and some necessary new material written in.
First performed: Open Space, 26 May 1971 (dir. Charles Marowitz, des. John Napier, with Timothy West as Gilbert, Peter Davies as Ernest).
First published: in *Plays and Players*, Oct. 1971, p. 64-72.

'A theory of aesthetics which is, at the same time, a philosophy of life. . . . Today I am prepared to defend almost all its ideas.' So says Marowitz in 'A Play Postscript', *Plays and Players*, Oct. 1971, p. 73, where he states his aim of staging the treatise as 'an elaborate kind of intellectual seduction'.

Oscar Wilde left a considerable body of work in a variety of forms. The publication of most of it within a period of little over six years, especially in 1891 and 1894, partly accounts for its close interrelatedness. Detractors of the doctrine of 'art for art's sake' rarely do justice to the seriousness and subtlety of Wilde's interpretation of it in theory, criticism, and the imaginative writings which he claimed as his mode of thought. The art to which he was dedicated was an idealization of life, an expression of soul, a form of creative being. Turning his back on fashionable 'realism' to cultivate style and personality was part of his attempt to introduce a unity where his contemporary and compatriot, W. B. Yeats, was to see a cruel choice between 'Perfection of the life, or of the work'. The temptation most critics have felt to read prophesies of Wilde's destiny in his imaginative writings was anticipated by his own claim, in *De Profundis*, to have lived in a symbolic relationship to his time.

On leaving Oxford, he had to make a living. Lecturing and journalism — reporting other people's lectures, as well as reviewing their books — were ways of doing so which also allowed him to work out his ideas and establish his place in contemporary intellectual and cultural life. Gifted with a fine mind, an outstanding student of the Classics, especially Greek, widely read — in German idealist philosophy as well as in poetry and drama — he cultivated his visual sensibility and made his first impact on the general public as a self-appointed arbiter of dress and interior decoration: the man of taste as artist. He joined Whistler, the American-born artist who had lived in Paris, in resurrecting the eighteenth-century beau as dandy, cultivating lightness of touch, what he called 'triviality', and evanescent brilliance in conversation. W. S. Gilbert's mockery of aestheticism, in the comic opera *Patience* (1881), gave him wider publicity with inevitable distortion of his purpose. Wilde's rebellion against Victorian ugliness was accompanied by rejection of heavy Victorian moralism and the repression of the human spirit by economic and social structures associated with puritanism. He identified himself with the aristocracy and espoused socialism in the spirit of Rossetti, Ruskin, and Morris as a condition of universal individual self-fulfilment, aristocracy for all.

Inevitably, given his background and his mother's example, he had to write poetry, and his first published book was *Poems* (1881). Contemporary reviewers brought him to task for imitativeness, even plagiarism. He was certainly a very literary poet, writing consciously within the double tradition of classical Greek subjects and romantic perceptions and treatment deriving above all from Keats. He absorbed French influences, especially Gautier and Flaubert. Technically, his decorative, cloyingly sensuous writing, loaded with images from visual art, and sophisticated in its prosody, cultivates exotic forms of beauty. His personal vacillation between scepticism and faith made him receptive to the symbols of alien and older religions which fascinated other late nineteenth-century poets and scholars. This poetry is little to our modern taste, poetry as luxury, defiantly expressive of a decadent culture, showing art as ostentatious wealth, implying the oppression of common humanity for the delectation of the few, and recognizing the savour of such cruelty as the ultimate passion. The sado-masochistic vein links the poems with *Salomé* and *The Picture of Dorian Gray*.

The study of ancient Greek culture in the spirit of romantic idealism suffused the nineteenth-century idea of the university. In his life as art, Wilde acted out devotion to the beauty of the young male in the person of Lord Alfred Douglas. In 'The Portrait of Mr. W. H.', he eroticized the relation between writer and muse, playwright and interpreter, in arguing for the identity of the 'onlie begetter' of Shakespeare's sonnets with a boy-player of female roles, for whom and in whose image the androgynous heroines of the plays were created. His separately published long poem *The Sphinx* employs the symbolism of ambiguous sex and species in a contemplation of the finally impenetrable nature of personal — and cultural — identity.

His prison experience led to the writing of *The Ballad of Reading Gaol*, generally considered his finest poem, as well as his most realistic. Its focal point is the expected execution of a murderer. Though the experiences and reflections the poem conveys have a new sombreness, it was not the first time that Wilde had been occupied with the study of a criminal and his crime: in 'Pen Pencil and Poison', one of the essays included in his great collection *Intentions*, he had pondered on the life and character of the notorious Wainewright to discover the similarities of artist and criminal. (He had not forsaken literary models: De Quincey's 'Murder Considered as a Fine Art' contributed to his thinking, as Coleridge's 'Rime of the Ancient Mariner' haunted his ear.)

Though Wilde asserted, 'In art, good intentions are not of the smallest value' the title, *Intentions*, in preference to the usual 'Essays', signifies a liking for floating ideas, rather than active endeavour. His major critical essays are theoretical and turn inconsistency into a valuable device. 'The Decay of Lying' and 'The Critic as Artist' were written in dialogue form, half-way to drama, on the principle that 'To arrive at what one really believes, one must speak through lips different from one's own'; not less remarkable is the charm of relaxed informality this gives the essays. Wilde's serious thinking on the critical function had started in Oxford, where he wrote a long essay on 'The Rise of Historical Criticism' and came under the influence of Walter Pater's *Studies in the Renaissance*. While in the USA, he profited from his early experience in art (and craft) journalism, and his familiarity with the contemporary London art scene, in a lecture on 'The English Renaissance in Art', and supplied a paradoxically named preface ('Envoi') on the principles of 'the modern romantic school' for a slim volume by his friend, Rennell Rodd. His interest in the theatre (evident in his inclusion of 'Impressions de Théâtre' in *Poems*) was demonstrated in the support he gave to E. W. Godwin on the desirability of historically accurate stage design, as considerable research in Elizabethan theatrical history and an ambivalent familiarity with the contemporary movement in Shakespeare criticism gave substance to his 'Portrait of Mr. W. H.'. 'The Decay of Lying', 'The Critic as Artist', the end of 'The Truth of Masks', and the aphoristic Preface to *The Picture of Dorian Gray*, mark a turning-point in the history of criticism in Britain. Walter Pater hailed him as successor to Matthew Arnold; Richard Ellmann has pointed out his anticipation of key twentieth-century insights, observing his twin recognitions that 'art is disengaged from actual life', but also 'deeply incriminated with it'. He views criticism as a creative art, a necessary self-consciousness in the artist, and a liberated responsibility of the receiver.

Yet *The Picture of Dorian Gray* and some of his *Tales* (e.g., 'The Young King' and 'The Fisherman and His Soul') embody a dialectic of aesthetic and ethical views. The end of 'The Truth of Masks', in which the author invokes Hegel's authority, carefully states: 'That only is a truth in art whose contradictory is also true.' That proposition can certainly be applied to narratives in which the central figures are convicted of excessive love of beauty (or the greed of luxury), and some are converted to the Christian value of self-sacrificing love. It is tempting to see the treatment of the Faust-motif and the element of gothic horror in *Dorian Gray* as returning to Victorian morality; but Wilde's epigrammatic Preface battles against such an interpretation, and 'The Devoted Friend' signs off with a graceful and humorous reflection on the danger of relating a story with a moral: if it does not succeed artistically, the teller would do better to save his breath. His first tales to be published, collected in *Lord Arthur Savile's Crime and Other Stories*, reflect and comment on contemporary society in a blend of ironic humour with varying proportions of fantasy, and show occasional affiliations with the tales of Henry James. The other collections follow in the wake of Hans Christian Andersen, but avoid his sentimentality. These later stories are more fabulous and more melancholy, and are increasingly concerned with suffering, redemption, and the getting of wisdom. Both the novel, *The Picture of Dorian Gray*, and these tales show a typically Wildean balance between idea and story, critical self-consciousness and spell-binding. (Walter Pater's *Imaginary Portraits* was among Wilde's models.) The proportions are different in the more condensed pieces published as *Poems in Prose* and which might as appropriately be termed parables.

Wilde the celebrated conversationalist seems to have been both a wit and an enthralling *raconteur*. Parables, scenarios for longer works, and versions of his tales were enjoyed by listeners and sometimes published later, sometimes not. Memories of his conversation thus became a source for 'reconstructions', the authenticity of which is often doubtful. Also in the extensive Wilde apocrypha is *Teleny*, 'a physiological romance of today', which has continued to be circulated as a homo-erotic classic, with Wilde's name attached.

The last prose work of substance that he wrote was the immensely long letter to Lord Alfred Douglas which he composed in prison and which is known as *De Profundis*. It is a combination of bitter love letter and *apologia pro vita sua* of much more than personal interest.

Journalism and Lectures

First published article, 'The Grosvenor Gallery', *Dublin University Review*, July 1877, included in *Miscellanies*, 1908.

Early in 1885, Wilde had a number of unsigned reviews published in *Pall Mall Gazette*, the *Dramatic Review* and other journals.

Between 1886 and 1888, about 100 of his reviews appeared in *Pall Mall Gazette*.

From 1887 to 1889 he contributed 'Literary and Other Notes' to the *Woman's World*.

He lectured in America, in 1882, on 'The English Renaissance of Art' (see 'Essays', below), 'The House Beautiful' and 'The Decorative Arts', and in England, in 1884, on 'Dress', 'The Value of Art in Modern Life', and 'Beauty, Taste and Ugliness in Dress'.

Texts were first collected in *Essays, Criticisms and Reviews*, 1901, and *Essays and Lectures*, ed. Ross, 1909; reprinted, New York: Garland, 1977.

A selection (including 'The Tomb of Keats', 'Mr. Whistler's Ten O'Clock', 'The Relation of Dress to Art', 'Ben Jonson', 'English Poetesses'), was published in *The Artist as Critic*, ed. R. Ellmann, 1970; another selection was made by S. Weintraub in *The Literary Criticism of Oscar Wilde*, 1968.

Poetry

Ravenna, Newdigate Prize Poem. Oxford: Thomas Shrimpton and Son, 1878. [Fraudulent imprint, actually published, London: Wright and Jones, 1904.]

'The Artist's Dream', translation of 100-line poem by the Polish actress, Helen Modjeska, *Routledge's Christmas Annual*, 1880.

Poems. David Bogue, 1882.

The Sphinx. Elkin Mathews and John Lane, 1894.

The Ballad of Reading Gaol. 'By C.3.3.', 1898; reprinted with Wilde's name attached, and with shorter version based on original draft, Methuen, 1910.

Essays

'The Rise of Historical Criticism', written at Oxford, 1879; first published 1908.

'The English Renaissance of Art', text of lecture given in New York, 1882; first published 1909.

'Envoi', preface to Rennel Rodd, *Rose Leaf and Apple Leaf*. Philadelphia: Stoddart, 1882.

'Shakespeare on Scenery', *Dramatic Review*, 14 March 1885.

'Shakespeare and Stage Costume', *Nineteenth Century*, May 1885. [William Archer's response to this appeared in *Dramatic Review*, 23 May 1885.]

'Pen Pencil and Poison', *Fortnightly Review*, Jan. 1889.

'The Decay of Lying', *Nineteenth Century*, Jan. 1889.

'The True Function and Value of Criticism', *Nineteenth Century*, July and Sept. 1890.

'The Soul of Man under Socialism', *Fortnightly Review*, Feb. 1891.

Preface to *The Picture of Dorian Gray*, *Fortnightly Review*, March 1891.

Intentions. London: Osgood, McIlvaine, 1891; New York: Dodd, Mead, 1891. [Revised versions of earlier essays.]

See 'Fiction', below, for *The Portrait of Mr. W. H.* and 'Epigrams, Letters, and Notebooks' for *De Profundis*.

Fiction

'The Canterville Ghost', *Court and Society Review*, Feb. and March 1887.

'Lord Arthur Savile's Crime', *Court and Society Review*, May 1887.

'The Model Millionaire', *The World*, May 1887.

'Lady Alroy', *The World*, May 1887.

The Happy Prince and Other Tales. David Nutt, 1888. [Contains 'The Happy Prince', 'The Selfish Giant', 'The Nightingale and the Rose', 'The Devoted Friend', 'The Remarkable Rocket'.]

'The Young King', *The Lady's Pictorial*, Christmas number, 1888.

'The Birthday of the Infanta', *Paris Illustré*, March 1889.

'The Portrait of Mr. W. H.', *Blackwood's Edinburgh Magazine*, July 1889; second, longer version first published in book form, Duckworth, 1921. [This version elaborates the theory and gives more prominence to the narrator.]

The Picture of Dorian Gray, novel, first published in *Lippincott's Monthly Magazine*, June 1890; in book form, enlarged and revised, Ward, Lock, 1891.

Lord Arthur Savile's Crime and Other Stories. Osgood, McIlvaine, 1891 [Contains revised versions of first four stories in this section.]

A House of Pomegranates. Osgood, McIlvaine, 1891. [Includes the previously unpublished items, 'The Fisherman and His Soul' and 'The Star-Child'.]

Teleny, or *The Reverse of the Medal*. Cosmopoli (in fact privately printed for Leonard Smithers and attributed to Oscar Wilde), 1893, two vols; expurgated version ed. H. Montgomery Hyde, 1966; ed. with introduction by John McRae, 1986, attributed to 'Oscar Wilde and Others'.

'Poems in Prose', *Fortnightly Review*, July 1894. [Contains revised versions of 'The House of Judgment' and 'The Disciple' which had previously appeared in *The Spirit Lamp*, Feb. and June 1893; also 'The Artist', 'The Doer of Good', 'The Master'.]

Epigrams, Letters, and Notebooks

'A Few Maxims for the Instruction of the Over-Educated', in *Miscellanies*, 1908.

'Phrases and Philosophies for the Use of the Young', *Chameleon*, I, No. 1, Dec. 1894.

The Epigrams of Oscar Wilde, ed. Owen Dudley Edwards, 1989.

De Profundis. Abridged version, 1905; first complete version, 1949. The best text is in *Letters*. [Title due to Robert Ross, who substituted it for Wilde's 'In Carcere et Vinculis'.]

Letters, ed. Rupert Hart-Davis, 1963.

More Letters, ed. R. Hart-Davis, 1985.

Oscar Wilde's Oxford Notebooks, ed. Philip E. Smith II and Michael S. Helfand, 1988.

Oscar Wilde chose to speak much oftener as the Artist, or Critic, in general terms, than personally and directly about his own work, though he occasionally laid the mask aside with an arresting flourish. As awareness of his aesthetic standpoint is essential to an understanding of his plays and other writings, a key selection of his general aesthetic pronouncements is given here, followed by relevant remarks about the specific art of drama, acting, and the theatre, and more personal comments about himself as author.

On Art in General

What is the use of telling artists that they should try and paint Nature as she really is? What Nature really is, is a question for metaphysics, not for art. Art deals with appearances, and the eye of the man who looks at Nature, the vision of the artist, is far more important to us than what he looks at.

> Unsigned review, 1889, reprinted in
> *The Artist as Critic* (W. H. Allen, 1970), p. 127

What Art really reveals to us is Nature's lack of design, her curious crudities, her extraordinary monotony, her absolutely unfinished condition. . . . Art is our spirited protest, our gallant attempt to teach Nature her proper place.

> Vivian, in the dialogue, 'The Decay of Lying',
> reprinted in *The Artist as Critic*, p. 291

Art takes life as part of her rough material, recreates it, and refashions it in fresh forms, is absolutely indifferent to fact, invents, imagines, dreams, and keeps between herself and reality the impenetrable barrier of beautiful style, of decorative or ideal treatment.

> Vivian, as above, p. 301

Art never expresses anything but itself. This is the principle of my new aesthetics . . . and it is this . . . that makes music the type of all the arts.

> Vivian, as above, p. 313-14

The highest art rejects the burden of the human spirit, and gains more from a new medium or a fresh material than she does from any enthusiasm for art, or from any lofty passion, or from any great awakening of the human consciousness.

Vivian, as above, p. 314

Those who do not love Beauty more than Truth never know the inmost shrine of Art.

Vivian, as above, p. 318

A mask tells us more than a face.

'Pen, Pencil and Poison', reprinted in
The Artist as Critic, p. 323

Art's final appeal is neither to the intellect nor to the emotions, but purely to the artistic temperament. . . .

As above, p. 326

To reveal art and conceal the artist is art's aim. . . .

There is no such thing as a moral or immoral book. Books are well written or badly written. That is all. . . .

The moral life of man forms part of the subject-matter of the artist, but the morality of art consists in the perfect use of an imperfect medium.

No artist desires to prove anything. Even things that are true can be proved.

No artist has ethical sympathy. An ethical sympathy in an artist is an unpardonable mannerism of style. . . .

Thought and language are to the artist instruments of an art. . . .

From the point of view of form, the type of all the arts is the art of the musician. From the point of view of feeling the actor's craft is the type. . . .

It is the spectator, and not life, that art really mirrors. . . .

All art is quite useless.

Preface to *The Picture of Dorian Gray*,
in *Plays, Prose Writings, and Poems*, p. 69-70

The further away the subject-matter is, the more freely can the artist work. . . . An artist . . . has no ethical sympathies at all. Virtue and wickedness are to him simply what the colours on his palette are to the painter. . . . He sees that by their means a certain artistic effect can be produced, and he produces it.

> Letter to Editor of *Scots Observer*, 9 July 1890,
> reprinted in *Letters*, p. 247-8

Without the critical faculty, there is no artistic creation at all, worthy of the name. . . . That fine spirit of choice and delicate instinct of selection, by which the artist realizes life for us, and gives to it a momentary perfection . . . is really the critical faculty in one of its most characteristic moods.

> Gilbert in 'The Critic as Artist', I, reprinted in
> *Plays, Prose Writings, and Poems*, p. 16

Dialogue . . . that wonderful literary form which . . . the creative critics of the world have always employed, can never lose for the thinker its attraction as a mode of expression. By its means he can both reveal and conceal himself. . . . By such means he can exhibit the object from each point of view, and show it to us in the round, as a sculptor shows us things. . . . To arrive at what one really believes, one must speak through lips different from one's own.

> As above, p. 49

Aesthetics are higher than ethics. They belong to a more spiritual sphere.

> As above, p. 63

Not that I agree with everything that I have said in this essay. There is much with which I entirely disagree. The essay simply represents an artistic standpoint, and in aesthetic criticism attitude is everything. For in art there is no such thing as a universal truth. A truth in art is that whose contradictory is also true. And just as it is only in art-criticism, and through it, that we can apprehend the Platonic theory of ideas, so it is only in art-criticism, and through it, that we can realize Hegel's system of contraries. The truths of metaphysics are the truths of masks.

> 'The Truth of Masks', in *The Artist as Critic*, p. 432

A work of art is the unique result of a unique temperament. Its beauty comes from the fact that the author is what he is. It has nothing to do

with the fact that other people want what they want. [Wilde's italics.]
'The Soul of Man under Socialism',
in *Plays, Prose Writings, and Poems*, p. 270

Statements on Drama, its Medium and Practice.

All good plays are a combination of the dream of a poet and that practical knowledge of the actor which gives concentration to action, which intensifies situation, and for poetic effect, which is description, substitutes dramatic effect, which is Life.

To Mary Anderson, Sept. 1882, in *Letters*, p. 125

In a play the characters should create each other: no character must be ready made. . . .

An audience longs to be first out of sympathy, and ultimately in sympathy, with a character they have loved . . . but *this sympathy must not be merely emotional, it must have its intellectual basis*, above all it must be summed up for them briefly in the form of thought: audiences are well meaning but very stupid: they must have things told them clearly: they are nice children who need to have their vague emotions crystallized and expressed for them. . . . This intellectual idea is the health of art, as the emotional idea is the heart of art.

To Mary Anderson, 23 Mar. 1883, in *Letters*, p. 139

As regards dialogue, you can produce tragic effects by introducing comedy. A laugh in an audience does not destroy terror, but, by relieving it, aids it. Never be afraid that by raising a laugh you destroy tragedy. On the contrary, you intensify it. The canons of each art depend on what they appeal to. . . . The drama appeals to human nature, and must have as its ultimate basis the science of psychology and physiology. Now, one of the facts of physiology is the desire of any very intensified emotion to be relieved by some emotion that is its opposite. Nature's example of dramatic effect is the laughter of hysteria or the tears of joy. So I cannot cut out my comedy lines. Besides, the essence of good dialogue is interruption. All good dialogue should give the effect of its being made by the reaction of the personages on one another. . . .

To Marie Prescott, March-April 1883, in *Letters*, p. 143

A ready-made character is not necessarily either mechanical or wooden. . . . If a character in a play is life-like . . . we have no right to insist on the author explaining its genesis to us. We must accept it as it is; and in the hands of a good dramatist mere presentation can take the place of analysis, and indeed is often a more dramatic method, because a more direct.

'Ben Jonson', unsigned review in *Pall Mall Gazette*, 20 Sept. 1886, reprinted in *The Artist as Critic*, p. 35

The aim of social comedy . . . is to mirror the manners, not to reform the morals of its day, and the censure of the Puritan, whether real or affected, is always out of place in literary criticism, and shows a want of recognition of the essential distinction between art and life . . . and there is very little use in airing one's moral sense at the expense of one's artistic appreciation.

'Mr. Mahaffy's New Book', unsigned review in *Pall Mall Gazette*, 9 Nov. 1887, reprinted in *The Artist as Critic*, p. 83

To Shakespeare, the actor was a deliberate and self-conscious fellow worker who gave form and substance to a poet's fancy, and brought into Drama the elements of a noble realism. . . . The actor could become, though it were but for a moment, a creative artist, and touch by his mere presence and personality those springs of terror and of pity to which tragedy appeals. This full recognition of the actor's art, and of the actor's power, was one of the things that distinguished the Romantic from the Classical Drama, and one of the things, consequently, that we owed to Shakespeare.

'The Portrait of Mr. W.H.', reprinted in *The Artist as Critic*, p. 180

All Art has its medium, its material . . . and, as one of the most fascinating critics of our day has pointed out, it is to the qualities inherent in each material, and special to it, that we owe the sensuous element in Art, and with [it] all that in Art is essentially artistic. . . . What of the Actor, who is the medium through which alone the Drama can truly reveal itself? Surely, in that strange mimicry of life by the living which is the mode and method of theatric art, there are sensuous elements of beauty that none of the other arts possess. Looked at from one point of view, the common players of the saffron-strewn stage are Art's most complete, most satisfying instruments. There is no passion in bronze, nor motion in marble. The sculptor must surrender colour, and the painter fullness of form. . . . It is the Drama only that . . . uses all means at once, and . . . has . . . in its service, form and colour, tone, look, and word, the swiftness of motion, the intense realism of visible action. . . .

It may be that in this very completeness of the instrument lies the secret of some weakness in the art. Those arts are happier that employ a material remote from reality, and there is a danger in the absolute identity of medium and matter, the danger of ignoble realism and unimaginative imitation.

As above, p. 182-3

Shakespeare himself was a player, and wrote for players. . . . He created parts that can be only truly revealed to us on the stage, wrote plays that need the theatre for their full realization. . . .

As above, p. 183

To say that only a woman can portray the passions of a woman . . . is to rob the art of acting of all claim to objectivity, and to assign to the mere accident of sex what properly belongs to imaginative insight and creative energy.

As above, p. 192

The theatre-going public like the obvious, it is true, but they do not like the tedious; and burlesque and farcical comedy, the two most popular art forms, are distinct works of art. Delightful work may be produced under burlesque and farcical conditions, and in work of this kind the artist in England is allowed very great freedom. It is when one comes to the higher forms of the drama that the result of popular control is seen. The one thing that the public dislike is novelty. . . and yet the vitality and progress of art depend in a large measure on the continual extension of subject-matter. . . . The public dislike novelty because they are afraid of it. It represents to them a mode of Individualism, an assertion on the part of the artist that he selects his own subject, and treats it as he chooses.

'The Soul of Man under Socialism', reprinted in
Plays, Prose Writings, and Poems, p. 272

As a certain advance has been made in the drama within the last ten or fifteen years, it is important to point out that this advance is entirely due to a few individual artists refusing to accept the popular want of taste as their standard, and refusing to regard Art as a mere matter of demand and supply.

As above, p. 278

A great work of dramatic art should not merely be made expressive of modern passion by means of the actor, but should be presented to us in the form most suitable to the modern spirit. . . . Perfect accuracy of detail, for the sake of perfect illusion, is necessary for us. What we have to see is that the details are not allowed to usurp the principal place. They must be subordinate always to the general motive of the play.

'The Truth of Masks', reprinted in The Artist as Critic, p. 425

Neither in costume nor in dialogue is beauty the dramatist's primary aim at all. The true dramatist aims first at what is characteristic. . . . The true dramatist, in fact, shows us life under the conditions of art, not art in the form of life.

As above, p. 428

The actable value of a play has nothing whatever to do with its value as a work of art. . . .

The mere suggestion that stage representation is any test of a work of art is quite ridiculous.

Letter to the Editor of the Daily Telegraph, 19 Feb. 1892,
reprinted in Letters, p. 310

When a play that is a work of art is produced on the stage, what is being tested is not the play, but the stage; when a play that is not a work of art is produced on the stage what is being tested is not the play, but the public.

Interview, St. James's Gazette, 18 Jan. 1895, reprinted in
More Letters, ed. R. Hart-Davis (London: John Murray), 1985, p. 195

In literature we require distinction, charm, beauty, and imaginative power. We don't want to be harrowed and disgusted with accounts of the lower orders.

Vivian in 'The Decay of Lying',
reprinted in The Artist as Critic, p. 296

Personal Statements on His Own Work

[*On his poems specifically:*] You dare to do, what I hardly dare, to sing of the passion and joy and sorrow of the lives of men and women among whom we live. . . .

For my own part I fear I too often 'trundle back my soul five hundred years', as Aurora Leigh says, and find myself more at home in the woods of Colonus or the glades of Arcady than I do in this little fiery-coloured world of ours. I envy you your strength. I have not got it.

To Clement Scott, *c.* Sept. 1880, reprinted in *Letters*, p. 69-70

I send you a copy of my drama which you were kind enough to hear me read some months ago; any suggestions about situations or dialogue I should be so glad to get from such an experienced artist as yourself: I have just found out what a difficult craft playwriting is.

To Hermann Vezin, 4 Oct. 1880, reprinted in *Letters*, p. 71

I have finished two plays. This sounds ambitious, but we live in an age of inordinate personal ambition and I am determined that the world shall understand me, so I will now, along with my art work, devote to the drama a great deal of my time. The drama seems to me to be the meeting place of art and life.

To Clarisse Moore, *c.* April-May 1883, reprinted in *Letters*, p. 146

My plays are difficult to produce well: they require artistic setting on the stage, a good company that knows something of the style essential to high comedy, beautiful dresses, a sense of the luxury of modern life. . . .

To Grace Hawthorne, 4 Oct. 1894, reprinted in *Letters*, p. 374

Between me and life there is a mist of words. I throw probability out of the window for the sake of a phrase, and the chance of an epigram makes me desert truth. Still I do aim at making a work of art, and I am really delighted that you think my treatment subtle and artistically good.

To Arthur Conan Doyle, April 1891, reprinted in *Letters*, p. 291-2

You knew what my art was to me, the great primal note by which I had revealed, first myself to myself, and then myself to the world.

To Lord Alfred Douglas, *De Profundis*,
reprinted in *Letters*, p. 447

I was a man who stood in symbolic relations to the art and culture of my age.

As above, p. 466

I made art a philosophy and philosophy an art: I altered the minds of men and the colours of things. . . . I took the drama, the most objective form known to art, and made it as personal a mode of expression as the lyric or sonnet; at the same time I widened its range and enriched its characterization. Drama, novel, poem in prose, poem in rhyme, subtle or fantastic dialogue, whatever I touched, I made beautiful in a new mode of beauty: to truth itself I gave what is false no less than what is true as its rightful province, and showed that the false and the true are merely forms of intellectual existence. I treated art as the supreme reality. . . . I summed up all systems in a phrase and all existence in an epigram.

As above, p. 466

Primary Sources

The place of publication is London, unless otherwise stated.

Collections

Collected Works, edited by Robert Ross, fifteen volumes. London: Methuen, limited edition, 1908-1922; trade edition, 1909-1922; reprinted, 1969. [Uniform edition, with no general title or volume numbers.]

The Portable Oscar Wilde, edited with introduction by Richard Aldington. New York: Viking Press, 1946; reprinted, Harmondsworth: Penguin, 1977. [Contains: 'The Critic as Artist', *The Picture of Dorian Gray*, *Salomé*, *The Importance of Being Earnest*, *De Profundis*, selected poems, poems in prose, some letters, etc.]

The Works, edited by G. F. Maine. London and Glasgow: Collins, 1948.

Complete Works, edited by J. B. Foreman. London and Glasgow: Collins, 1966. [The original four-act version of *The Importance of Being Earnest* is included in this edition and subsequent reprints.]

The Letters of Oscar Wilde, edited by Rupert Hart-Davis. Hart-Davis, 1962.

The Literary Criticism of Oscar Wilde, edited with introduction by Stanley Weintraub. Lincoln, Nebraska: University of Lincoln Press, 1968 [Regents Critics series.]

The Artist as Critic: Critical Writings of Oscar Wilde, edited by Richard Ellmann. W. H. Allen, 1970; University of Chicago Press, 1982.

Plays, Prose Writings, and Poems, with an introduction by Isobel Murray. London: Dent, 1975. [An Everyman's Library selection, including 'The Critic as Artist', *The Picture of Dorian Gray*, *The Soul of Man under Socialism*, *Lady Windermere's Fan*, *The Importance of Being Earnest*, *The Ballad of Reading Gaol*, 'The Harlot's House', 'The Sphinx', 'A Few Maxims for the Instruction of the Over-Educated', etc.]

Selected Letters, edited by Rupert Hart-Davis. Hart-Davis, 1979.

The Complete Shorter Fiction, edited by Isobel Murray. Oxford University Press, 1979.

More Letters of Oscar Wilde, edited by Rupert Hart-Davis. John Murray, 1985.

The Complete Plays, edited with introduction by H. Montgomery Hyde. Methuen, 1988. [The Gribsby scene from the four-act version of *The Importance of Being Earnest* is given in an appendix.]

Oscar Wilde, edited by Isobel Murray. Oxford and New York: Oxford University Press, 1989. [A generous, annotated selection of texts in the 'Oxford Authors' series, based on the final versions seen through the press by Wilde himself. The contents differ from the Everyman Library selection in the omission of *The Soul of Man under Socialism*, but the addition of *Salomé, An Ideal Husband*, three tales, and one more poem in prose. Despite resemblances, the introductions to the two collections are distinct and both worth reading.]

The Epigrams of Oscar Wilde, edited by Owen Dudley Edwards. Barrie and Jenkins, 1989.

Noteworthy Editions of Single Works

Salomé. Paris: Elkin Mathews and John Lane, 1893. [First publication of original French text.]

Salomé and A Florentine Tragedy, with introduction by Robert Ross, reprinted, Methuen, 1969. [Contains Wilde's original French text of *Salomé*.]

De Profundis, edited with introduction by Vyvyan Holland. Methuen, 1949. [First publication of complete text.]

The Importance of Being Earnest, edited with introduction by Sara Augusta Dickson. New York Public Library, Arents Tobacco Collection, Publication No. 6, 1956. [In two volumes: first publication of the four-act version.]

The Original Four-Act Version of The Importance of Being Earnest, edited with introduction by Vyvyan Holland. Methuen, 1957.

Vera, edited by Frances Miriam Reed. Lewiston: Edwin Mellen Press, 1989.

The Picture of Dorian Gray, edited by Isobel Murray. Oxford: Oxford University Press, 1974; reprinted 1979. [Oxford English Novels.]

The Importance of Being Earnest, edited by Russell Jackson. London: Benn; New York: Norton, 1980. [New Mermaid series.]

Lady Windermere's Fan, edited by Ian Small. London: Benn; New York: Norton, 1980. [New Mermaid series.]

Two Society Comedies (*A Woman of No Importance* and *An Ideal Husband*), edited by Ian Small and Russell Jackson. London: Benn; New York: Norton, 1983. [New Mermaid series.]

The Picture of Dorian Gray, edited by Donald L. Lawler. New York: Norton Critical Editions, 1988.

Oscar Wilde's Oxford Notebooks, edited by Philip E. Smith II and
  Michael S. Helfand. New York: Oxford University Press, 1988.

Dramatized Scenario

Frank Harris, *Mr. and Mrs. Daventry*, edited by H. Montgomery Hyde.
  Richards Press, 1956. [Play based on scenario by Wilde, edited from
  text in Lord Chamberlain's collection, now in British Library.]

Secondary Sources

Biographical Works

*Most publications on Wilde, up to the present, have been largely
concerned with his life and personality. What follows here is a selective
list of accounts by his contemporaries and associates, followed by the
principal more recent and objective biographical studies.*

Oscar Wilde: a Study from the French of André Gide, with introduction,
  notes, and bibliography by Stuart Mason [pseudonym of C. S.
  Merrill). Oxford: Holywell Press, 1905.
Frank Harris, *Life and Confessions of Oscar Wilde*. New York: Crown
  Publishing Company, 1930; new edition, entitled *Oscar Wilde, His
  Life and Confessions*, with introduction by Bernard Shaw, Constable,
  1938. [Notoriously fantastic and highly readable.]
Ada Leverson, ed., *Letters to the Sphinx from Oscar Wilde and
  Reminiscences of the Author*. Duckworth, 1930.
Jean Paul Raymond and Charles Ricketts, *Oscar Wilde: Recollections*.
  Nonesuch Press, 1932. ['Jean Paul Raymond' was a pseudonym
  adopted by Ricketts. The text includes material on plans for staging
  Salomé.]
Vincent O'Sullivan, *Aspects of Wilde*. Constable, 1936.
Alfred Douglas, *Oscar Wilde: a Summing Up*. Duckworth, 1940;
  reprinted 1962. [The last and most moderate of Douglas's accounts of
  his relationship with Wilde.]
Frances Winwar, *Oscar Wilde and the Yellow Nineties*. New York and
  London: Harper, 1940; second edition, with self-defensive foreword
  by Lord Alfred Douglas, Garden City, New York: Blue Ribbon
  Books, 1941.

Hesketh Pearson, *The Life of Oscar Wilde*. Methuen, 1954; reprinted
   several times. [The first balanced account: Pearson was a professional
   biographer who had been an actor in the Edwardian theatre.]
The Trials of Oscar Wilde, edited by H. Montgomery Hyde. William
   Hodge, 1948.
H. Montgomery Hyde, *Oscar Wilde*. New York: Da Capo, 1975;
   London: Eyre Methuen, 1976. [Includes extensive bibliography.]
Richard Ellmann, 'A Victorian Love Story', in John Espey, *Oscar
   Wilde: Two Approaches*, 1977. [See below, p. 78.]
Vyvyan Holland, *Oscar Wilde and His World*. Thames and Hudson,
   1978.
Oscar Wilde: Interviews and Recollections, edited by E. H. Mikhail,
   two vols. London: Macmillan, 1979.
Richard Ellmann, *Oscar Wilde*. London: Hamish Hamilton, 1987.
Oscar Wilde File, compiled by Jonathan Goodman. W. H. Allen, 1988.
   [An illustrated documentary reconstruction of Wilde's triumph and
   fall. Includes programmes and reviews of first productions.]

*Although their focus is oblique to Oscar Wilde himself, the following
items also claim mention here:*

Margery Ross, ed., *Robert Ross, Friend of Friends*. London: Jonathan
   Cape, 1952. [Letters, and extracts from articles.]
Vyvyan Holland, *Son of Oscar Wilde*. Hart-Davis, 1954.
Rupert Croft-Cooke, *Bosie*. Indianapolis and New York, 1963; London:
   New English Library, 1965.
Terence de Vere White, *The Parents of Oscar Wilde*. Hodder and
   Stoughton, 1967.
Ann Clark Amor, *Mrs. Oscar Wilde*. Sidgwick and Jackson, 1983.

Critical and Other Studies

William Archer, *The Theatrical 'World' for 1893*. Walter Scott, 1894.
William Archer, *The Theatrical 'World' for 1895*. Walter Scott, 1896.
William Archer, *Play-Making*. Chapman and Hall, 1912. [Analyzes a
   section of *Lady Windermere's Fan*.]
Max Beerbohm, *Around Theatres*, two vols. Heinemann, 1924.
Max Beerbohm, *More Theatres*. Hart-Davis, 1969.
Max Beerbohm, *Last Theatres*. Hart-Davis, 1970.
Clement Scott, *The Theatre of Yesterday and To-Day*, two vols.
   Macmillan, 1899.

G. B. Shaw, *Our Theatres in the Nineties*, two vols. Constable, 1932.

C. E. Montague, *Dramatic Values*. Methuen, 1911; Garden City, New York: Doubleday, Page, 1925; reprinted, Chatto and Windus, 1941.

St. John Hankin, 'Wilde as a Dramatist', in *The Dramatic Works of St. John Hankin*, Vol. III, p. 185-201. Martin Secker, 1912.

Arthur Ransome, *Oscar Wilde: a Critical Study*. Methuen, 1911; Martin Secker, 1912. [The earliest critical monograph.]

P. P. Howe, *Dramatic Portraits*. Martin Secker, 1913.

Holbrook Jackson, *The Eighteen Nineties*. Grant Richards, 1913.

Rose F. Egan, 'The Genesis of the Theory of "Art for Art's Sake" in Germany and England', *Smith College Studies in Modern Languages*, July 1921 and Apr. 1924.

Arthur Symons, *A Study of Oscar Wilde*. Charles Sawyer, 1930.

Mario Praz, *The Romantic Agony*. Oxford University Press, 1933; second edition, 1951.

Kelver Hartley, *Oscar Wilde: L'Influence française dans son oeuvre*. Paris: Librairie du Receuil Sirey, 1935.

James Agate, *First Nights*. Nicolson and Watson, 1934.

A. E. W. Mason, *Sir George Alexander and the St. James Theatre*. Macmillan, 1935; reprinted, New York and London: Blom, 1969. [Mason was an actor who worked with Alexander, before becoming a highly successful novelist.]

Janko Lavrin, *Aspects of Modernism: from Wilde to Pirandello*. Stanley Nott, 1935.

R. Snider, *Satire in the Comedies of Congreve, Sheridan, Wilde, and Noel Coward*. Orono: University of Maine Studies, Second Series, No. 42, 1937.

H. T. E. Perry, *Masters of Dramatic Comedy and Their Social Themes*. Cambridge, Mass.: Harvard University Press, 1939.

Charles Ricketts, *Self-Portrait*, from the Letters and Journals, compiled by T. Sturge Moore, ed. Cecil Lewis. Peter Davies, 1939. [On the productions of *A Florentine Tragedy* and *Salomé*.]

Arthur Nethercot, 'Oscar Wilde and the Devil's Advocate', *PMLA*, LIX, 1944.

William Gaunt, *The Aesthetic Adventure*. Jonathan Cape, 1945.

Eric Bentley, *The Playwright as Thinker*. New York: Reynal and Hitchcock, 1946; first published in Britain as *The Modern Theatre*, Robert Hale, 1948. [A turning-point in the appraisal of *The Importance of Being Earnest*.]

Cleanth Brooks and R. B. Heilman, *Understanding Drama*. Harrap, 1947. [Examines *Lady Windermere's Fan*.]

James Agate, 'Oscar Wilde and the Theatre', *The Masque*, No. 3 (Curtain Press, 1947). [Touches of virulence. Illustrated with designs for several productions.]

W. Macqueen Pope, *Haymarket: Theatre of Perfection*. W. H. Allen, 1948.

Graham Hough, *The Last Romantics*. Duckworth, 1949.

George Woodcock, *The Paradox of Oscar Wilde*. T. V. Boardman, 1950. [An anarchist viewpoint.]

St. John Ervine, *Oscar Wilde: a Present Time Appraisal*. Allen and Unwin, 1951. [Unsympathetic criticism of the plays as realistic structures from a well-known playwright and theatre critic of *The Observer*.]

Juan Luis Borges, 'About Oscar Wilde', *Other Inquisitions, 1937-1952*. London: Souvenir Press, 1973.

Tyrone Guthrie, Introduction to Oscar Wilde, *Plays* (Collins Modern Library edition, 1954). [A dated and limited view, but interesting as comments by a leading director.]

Allan Harris, 'Oscar Wilde as Playwright: a Centenary Review', *Adelphi*, XXX, No. 3, 1954.

I. Singer, 'The Aesthetics of "Art for Art's Sake",' *Journal of Aesthetics and Art Criticism*, XII, No. 3, Mar. 1954.

Kingsley Amis, Introduction to Oscar Wilde, *Poems and Essays* (Collins, 1956). [Characteristic observations by the poet and novelist.]

Edmund Bergler, '*Salomé*: Turning Point in Oscar Wilde's Life', *Psychoanalytic Review*, XLIII (1956), p. 97-103.

Otto Reinert, 'Satiric Strategy in *Earnest*', College English, XVIII, 1956.

Hesketh Pearson, *Beerbohm Tree*. Methuen, 1956; reprinted, Columbus Books, 1988.

Lennox Robinson, 'Oscar Wilde', in *I Sometimes Think*. Dublin: Talbot Press, 1956.

Alick West, *The Mountain and the Sunlight*. Lawrence and Wishart, 1958. [A distinguished Marxist critic discussing Wilde as a social thinker.]

W. Macqueen Pope, *St. James's: Theatre of Distinction*. W.H. Allen, 1958.

Arthur Ganz, 'The Divided Self in the Social Comedies of Oscar Wilde', *Modern Drama*, III, May 1960.

J. L. Styan, *Elements of Drama*. Cambridge University Press, 1960.

Hesketh Pearson, 'Oscar Wilde and His Actors', *Theatre Arts*, XLV Feb. 1961.

G. Wilson Knight, *The Golden Labyrinth*. Methuen, 1962. [Noteworthy for appraisal of *Vera*.]

John Gielgud, *Stage Directions*. Heinemann, 1963. [Includes an incomparable commentary on *The Importance of Being Earnest* as theatre.]

H. Toliver, 'Wilde and the Importance of Sincere and Studied Triviality', *Modern Drama*, V, 1963.

Barbara Charlesworth, *Dark Passages: the Decadent Consciousness in Victorian Literature*. Madison and Milwaukee: University of Wisconsin Press, 1965.

Susan Sontag, 'Notes on Camp', in *Against Interpretation*. New York: Farrar, Straus and Giroux, 1966. ['These Notes are for Oscar Wilde.']

Ian Gregor, 'Comedy and Oscar Wilde', *Sewanee Review*, 1966.

Richard Findlater, *Banned!* Macgibbon and Kee, 1967, p. 92-6.

Epifanio San Juan, Jr., *The Art of Oscar Wilde*. Princeton, N. J.: Princeton University Press, 1967.

Richard Ellmann, ed., *Twentieth Century Views of Oscar Wilde*. Englewood Cliffs, New Jersey: Prentice-Hall, 1969. [Includes items by Yeats, Gide, Pater, Lionel Johnson, Betjeman, Alfred Douglas, Hart Crane, James Joyce, Hankin, Thomas Mann, Borges, Behan.]

Frances Donaldson, *The Actor-Managers*. Weidenfeld and Nicholson, 1970, p. 110-12, 119-21.

K. Beckson, ed., *Oscar Wilde: the Critical Heritage*. Routledge and Kegan Paul, 1970. [Extracts from early critics.]

Kate Millett, *Sexual Politics*. Boston: New England Free Press, 1968; London: Hart-Davis, 1971. [Includes feminist discussion of *Salomé*.]

James M. Ware, 'Algernon's Appetite: Oscar Wilde's Hero as Restoration Dandy', *English Literature in Transition*, XIII, No. 1, 1970.

Ronald Hayman, *John Gielgud*. Heinemann, 1971.

John Stokes, *Resistible Theatres*. Elek, 1972.

Kevin Sullivan, *Oscar Wilde*. New York: Columbia University Press, 1972.

Christopher Nassaar, *Into the Demon Universe: a Literary Exploration of Oscar Wilde*. New Haven and London: Yale University Press, 1974.

Sheridan Morley, *Oscar Wilde*. Weidenfeld and Nicolson, 1976.

R. S. Pathak, *Oscar Wilde: a Critical Study*. Allahabad: Lokbharti, 1976. [Not seen.]

A. Bird, *The Plays of Oscar Wilde*. Vision Press, 1977.

Donald Erikson, *Oscar Wilde*. Boston, Mass.: Twayne, 1977. ['English Authors' series.]

Rodney Shewan, *Oscar Wilde: Art and Egotism*. Macmillan, 1977. [Apart from argument, valuable for its research.]

P. K. Cohen, *The Moral Vision of Oscar Wilde*. New Jersey and London: Associated University Presses, 1978.

John Stokes, *Oscar Wilde*. Harlow, Essex: Longman, for the British Council, 1978.

K. J. Worth, *The Irish Drama of Europe*. Athlone Press, 1978.

Ian Fletcher, ed., *Decadence and the 1890s*. Edward Arnold, 1979. [Stratford-upon-Avon Studies, 17.]

John Gielgud, *An Actor in His Time*. Sidgwick and Jackson, 1979.

Richard Cave, *Terence Gray and the Cambridge Festival Theatre*. Cambridge: Chadwyck-Healey; Teaneck, N. J.: Somerset House, 1980. ['Theatre in Focus' series: booklet accompanying slide set, including two slides of *Salomé*.]

Kate Terry Gielgud, *A Victorian Playgoer*, ed. M. St. Clare Byrne. Heinemann Educational, 1980. [A non-professional critic on early performances of *An Ideal Husband* and *A Woman of No Importance*.]

Oscar Wilde, Comedies: a Casebook. Macmillan, 1982.

Richard Pine, *Oscar Wilde*. Dublin: Gill and Macmillan, 1983.

K. J. Worth, *Oscar Wilde*. Macmillan, 1983. [Views Wilde as deploying popular theatrical conventions, as Shaw does, for an original purpose.]

Jean M. Ellis D'Alessandro, *Hues of Mutability: the Waning Vision in Oscar Wilde's Narrative*. Florence: University of Florence, 1984.

Regina Gagnier, *Idylls of the Market Place: Oscar Wilde and the Victorian Public*. Stanford: Stanford University Press, 1986; Aldershot: Scolar Press, 1987.

Peter Raby, *Oscar Wilde*. Cambridge University Press, 1988.

Steven Berkoff, Introduction to *Salomé*. Faber and Faber, 1989. [With reproductions of Beardsley's sardonic illustrations.]

For Further Reference

Stuart Mason [pseudonym of C. S. Millard], *A Bibliography of Oscar Wilde*. London: Werner Laurie, 1914; reprinted, Bertram Rota, 1967.

Ian Fletcher and John Stokes, 'Oscar Wilde', in *Anglo-Irish Literature: a Review of Research*, ed. R. J. Finneran. New York: Modern Language Association of America, 1976, p. 48-137. [Well-informed and valuable critical survey.]

E. H. Mikhail, *Oscar Wilde: an Annotated Bibliography of Criticism*. London: Macmillan, 1978. [Exhaustive listing.]

Ian Fletcher and John Stokes, 'Oscar Wilde', in *Recent Research on Anglo-Irish Writers*, ed. R. J. Finneran. New York: Modern Language Association of America, 1983, p. 21-47.

John Espey, 'Sources for Wilde Studies at the Clark Library', in *Oscar Wilde: Two Approaches*, intro. Robert Adams. Los Angeles: Clark Memorial Library, University of California, 1977, p. 25-48.